MERE
CALVINISM

MERE
CALVINISM

Jim Scott Orrick

P&R
P U B L I S H I N G
P.O. BOX 817 • PHILLIPSBURG • NEW JERSEY 08865-0817

Have any feedback on this book?
Write to P&R at editorial@prpbooks.com with your comments.
We'd love to hear from you.

Printed in the United States of America

Library of Congress Cataloging-in-Publication Data

Names: Orrick, Jim, 1960- author.
Title: Mere Calvinism / Jim Scott Orrick.
Description: Phillipsburg : P&R Publishing, 2019.
Identifiers: LCCN 2018046293 | ISBN 9781629956145 (pbk.) | ISBN 9781629956152 (epub) | ISBN 9781629956169 (mobi)
Subjects: LCSH: Calvin, Jean, 1509-1564. | Calvinism.
Classification: LCC BX9418 .O69 2019 | DDC 230/.42--dc23
LC record available at https://lccn.loc.gov/2018046293

To my uncle, Paul A. Orrick

CONTENTS

Introduction   9

1. Calvinism   13
   More Than the Five Points

2. Total Depravity   27
   We Have Received a Bleak Diagnosis

3. Unconditional Election   57
   The Father Planned for the Success of the Gospel

4. Limited Atonement   83
   The Son Secured the Salvation of His People

5. Irresistible Grace   133
   The Holy Spirit Supernaturally Calls the Elect

6. Perseverance of the Saints   161
   God Brings All His Children to Heaven

7. What If?   201
   Less Than the Five Points

Afterword   217

INTRODUCTION

Early in the 1990s, I was reading a book of literary criticism by C. S. Lewis when I came across an entire page on which Lewis discusses the influence of Calvinism in the sixteenth century. The sentence that caught my attention was this one: "Unless we can imagine the freshness, the audacity, and (soon) the fashionableness of Calvinism, we shall get our whole picture wrong." I was amazed that there had been a time when Calvinism was fashionable. I had been a Calvinist for virtually all my life, and I assure you that in the late twentieth century it was not fashionable to be a Calvinist. I knew a few older men who were Calvinists, but virtually no young people. Yet Lewis observed that in the writings of the sixteenth century, "Youth is the taunt commonly brought against the puritan leaders by their opponents: youth and cocksureness."[1] When I first read Lewis's words, I could barely have imagined that within twenty years I would see the time return when, in some circles, Calvinism would again become fashionable. Like before, many of the new Calvinists

---

1. C. S. Lewis, *English Literature in the Sixteenth Century Excluding Drama*, The Oxford History of English Literature 3 (Oxford: Oxford University Press, 1954), 43.

are young and cocksure. In many cases, however, their brash confidence is unfounded. Just because someone calls himself a Calvinist does not mean that he knows what Calvinism is.

For years I have preached in churches and taught in schools where many in my congregations and classrooms would have asserted that they were Calvinists. Or they might have said, "We are Reformed" or "We believe in the doctrines of grace." In many of those same congregations and classrooms, I have preached and taught through the material found in this book, and here is what I have observed: most of those persons who call themselves Calvinists do not really know much about Calvinism, and most of them are conscious of their ignorance. I tell my students that they are not going to be tested over the lectures, but they furiously take notes as if they have never before heard what I am saying. They ask intelligent but basic questions that reveal that some of them are working through these ideas and these Scriptures for the first time. Perhaps most revealing are the comments that I often get afterward: "I have been in this church/college for years, and I have never understood these doctrines until now." At the conclusion of the semester, I will sometimes poll my students, asking them, "If there has been a book, a lecture, or a discussion that has been especially helpful to you, I would like to hear about it." Far and away the most common response has been "The lectures on the Five Points of Calvinism."

When we first see the fundamental ideas of Calvinistic theology and recognize that the Bible is founded on the principle that God does as he pleases, we may rush to declare ourselves to be Calvinists, but we desperately hope that no one questions us carefully about what we believe. Worse, we get into arguments about the sovereignty of God, and we reveal our insecurity and immaturity by becoming angry with the people who disagree with us. I fear that we pastors and teachers are making a serious mistake when we assume that our people and students understand Calvinism just because they call themselves Calvinists.

I have attempted to write a simple, easy-to-understand explanation of the Five Points of Calvinism. I have tried to write a book that you might hand to a young Calvinist, or to someone who just wants to understand what Calvinism is, with the confidence that he or she will be able to understand the book. I have deliberately used a lot of illustrations that have helped me to understand these truths myself and explain them to others.

Several years ago, I announced to my classes that the following week I planned to lecture on the Five Points of Calvinism. Before the lectures, a student met me on campus, and with a concerned expression she asked, "Dr. Orrick, when you lecture on Calvinism, you *are* going to use the Bible, aren't you?" She went on to explain her question, observing that most of the discussions she had heard about Calvinism were more philosophical than biblical. I assured her that I would indeed use the Bible as the basis for everything I said, and I assure you of the same. You might read this book and think that I am misinterpreting the Bible, but if you are fair-minded, you will have to admit that I am trying to recognize and interpret what the Bible says. At least, that has been my goal.

Dr. Tom Nettles read the manuscript of this book and made several excellent suggestions, which I incorporated. Thank you. Years ago you told me to stop calling you "Dr. Nettles" and to call you by your first name, so I have. But I want you to know that, on the inside, I still call you "Dr. Nettles."

My wife Carol read the manuscript, and she too made valuable suggestions; and I incorporated nearly all of them. Thank you.

CALVINISM

More Than the Five Points

In Two Sentences, What Is a Calvinist?

The old farmer sitting across the table from me at the restaurant was not a troublemaker at church. In fact, he had been a peacemaker. It was he who had contacted me about becoming the interim pastor of the church where he had spent all of his eighty-plus years. The church was without a pastor because they had found it necessary to fire their former pastor, who by all accounts had proven himself to be an imprudent, impatient, pushy young upstart. He had very nearly split the church. He was a Calvinist.

I do not think it was his Calvinism that got him fired. I do not think so because, during the fifteen months that I served as interim pastor of that wonderful little church, I plainly preached the doctrines of God's sovereign grace as I encountered those truths again and again throughout a year-long exposition of Hebrews. During my ministry there, the church healed and grew, and when they called a full-time pastor and my ministry there concluded, I was deeply sad to leave a church I had come to love profoundly and whose strong love for me I had felt as well.

All those happy months of my ministry there were still future on that day when I sat across the table from the old farmer. In the absence of a pastor, he was the de facto leader of the church. I had preached at a nearby church during much of the preceding summer, and people from that church had recommended me to him. His church did not interview me before asking me to serve as their interim. I suppose they trusted the people who had recommended me. I also suppose that the farmer had only recently learned that I, their newly called interim pastor, was a Calvinist.

I imagine that when that wise, gracious farmer learned that I was a Calvinist, he must have thought, *Oh, no. A Calvinist preacher just came within a hair's breadth of destroying our church, and now, somehow, we have called another Calvinist to be our interim pastor.* I must surmise all this because, if he had these misgivings, he never let a word of it slip out of his mouth that day in the restaurant. Instead, without any prelude, he asked me, "In two sentences, what is a Calvinist?"

I answered something very close to this: "Well, in two sentences . . . First, a Calvinist believes that God always does whatever he pleases. Second, a Calvinist believes that God initiates, sustains, and completes the salvation of everyone who gets saved." The old farmer had a puzzled look, but he said nothing. I continued, "But probably what you want to know is whether Calvinists believe in missions and evangelism. The answer is yes." A big smile spread across his wizened, sunburnt face, and he said, "That's exactly what I wanted to know." That was the end of our conversation on Calvinism. Our food came, we enjoyed the meal, and as far as I remember, that was the only time anyone in that church ever spoke the word *Calvinist* to me; and I do not remember ever using the word in my preaching.

What Does the Bible Say?

I am not opposed to the word *Calvinism*. It is in the title of this book, and I will use it often. I start off this book on the Five Points of Calvinism with this little story in order that I might make the following preliminary observations about Calvinism.

To start, my aim in this book and in my entire preaching and teaching ministry is to explain what the Bible teaches—not to explain what John Calvin taught. I held to what is called Calvinist doctrine before I had read a single page of the writings of John Calvin.[1] I have since read some of Calvin's writings, and I greatly admire them. Should you ever read his commentaries or his *Institutes of the Christian Religion*, you will probably be pleasantly surprised at how readable and pastoral John Calvin is.[2]

I believe what I believe, however, not because John Calvin taught it, or because C. H. Spurgeon or one of my other heroes preached it, or because my parents reared me that way. I believe it because I am convinced that the Holy Spirit has revealed it in the Holy Bible. When he encounters controversial teaching in the Bible, a Bible teacher ought always to be able to point to the Scriptures and say, "I did not write this. I believe it because I believe the Bible, but I did not write this,

---

1. In fact, I was a Calvinist before I became a Christian; but I will say more about that later in this chapter.
2. The average person who is willing to put in the effort can understand the great classic books of Christianity, literature, and philosophy. The classics have become classics because average persons have read them for a very long time.

and this idea did not originate with me. We may not like what this text says; but, if Jesus is our teacher and our Lord, then we are bound to listen to what his Holy Spirit has said and are bound to receive it whether we fully understand it or not."

My goal in this book is to demonstrate to you, the reader, that the Bible teaches that God always does as he pleases, and that he initiates, sustains, and completes the salvation of everyone who goes to heaven. If after reading this book you honestly do not believe that what I write is taught in the Bible, then reject what I write. I hope you will prayerfully determine right now that you will carefully consider the biblical case I make for what I write, and that if you find that it is taught in the Bible, then you will embrace it as true. "To the teaching and to the testimony! If they will not speak according to this word, it is because they have no dawn" (Isa. 8:20).

I do not think that you must be a Calvinist to be a genuine Christian, but I do believe that you must submit to Christ as your trustworthy teacher and as your Lord. The teachings of the Lord have been given to us in the Bible, and if you see that an idea is clearly taught in the Bible, you are under obligation to receive it. You must never say, "I know that it is taught in the Bible, *but* . . ." When you see that the Lord has revealed something about himself and the way he acts, even if it is something that contradicts or challenges your long-cherished ideas about who God is, do not deflect the truth by saying, "My God is not like that" or "My God would never do that." If the Bible asserts something about God to be true, and it could not possibly be true of *your* God, then you have the wrong god.

A persistent reluctance to submit to the plain teaching of the Scripture is a sure indication that you have not repented of your sinful resolve to determine for yourself what is good and evil. You still have the forbidden fruit in your mouth. Spit it out and receive the words of Jesus: "Whoever hears my word and believes him who sent me has eternal life" (John 5:24). The focus of this book, then, is not to explain what John Calvin taught but to explain what the Bible teaches.

Calvinism Is More Than Five Points

Another point that my introductory story allows me to make is that Calvinism is more than the Five Points. Before we can make any significant progress toward determining the truthfulness of the Five Points, we need to understand that God always does as he pleases. Nearly every professing Christian who bases his faith on the Bible will acknowledge that God *may* do as he pleases—but the Bible asserts that God *does* do as he pleases. "His dominion is an everlasting dominion, and his kingdom endures from generation to generation; all the inhabitants of the earth are accounted as nothing, and he does according to his will among the host of heaven and among the inhabitants of the earth; and none can stay his hand or say to him, 'What have you done?'" (Dan. 4:34–35). While sinners may try to resist him, no one successfully resists him. God is the one "who works all things according to the counsel of his will" (Eph. 1:11).

As we are conformed to the likeness of Jesus and gain the mind of Christ, we learn not only to submit to God's sovereign rule in all things but also to submit cheerfully. We learn to say with our Savior, "I thank you, Father, Lord of heaven and earth, that you have hidden these things from the wise and understanding and revealed them to little children; yes, Father"—why?—"for such was your gracious will" (Matt. 11:25–26). No one but a true believer ever honestly tells God, "Thy will be done on earth as it is in heaven." Every true believer does say that to God. Cheerful, unconditional submission to the will of God is a condition of our admittance into his kingdom. We must be willing to say "Thy will be done," even when it comes to difficult teachings that may initially be unsettling.

Two simple statements in the Bible pave the way for everything else that the Bible says. If we believe these two statements, everything else is relatively easy to accept. The first one is the first verse of Genesis: "In the beginning, God created the heavens and the earth." If we believe this, then we believe that God made everything, and this gives him the power and the right to do anything he pleases. The second statement is Psalm 115:3: "Our God is in the heavens; he does all that he pleases." What God is pleased to do, he does do. Our main job is to learn to be pleased with what pleases God—to conform our will to his.

Since God is good, it is reasonable that his will is best; and since he is all wise, it also is reasonable that his will may sometimes be inscrutable to us. He reveals truths about himself that we could never figure out through our own wisdom. "In the wisdom of God, the world did not know God through wisdom" (1 Cor. 1:21). If we embrace only those doctrines of the Bible that accord with our unaided reason, we have not yet begun to exercise the kind of faith that the Holy Spirit identifies as the faith that results in salvation. For "faith is the assurance of things hoped for, the conviction of things not seen" (Heb. 11:1). Saving faith engages the truth that is above the grasp of mere human reason—the truth that God must reveal. When we receive this super-reasonable truth (this revealed truth that is above reason) and we receive the Christ who reveals it to us, we are "seeing him who is invisible" (Heb. 11:27) and can "know the love of Christ that surpasses knowledge" (Eph. 3:19).

We will encounter ideas about him that we cannot understand, for he is vastly superior to us. He says,

> For my thoughts are not your thoughts,
>> neither are your ways my ways, declares the Lord.
> For as the heavens are higher than the earth,
>> so are my ways higher than your ways
>> and my thoughts than your thoughts. (Isa. 55:8–9)

We ought to expect that such a wise and powerful God will have ways that are far above our ways. When we cannot understand why he does what he does, we must learn to reply,

> Oh, the depth of the riches and wisdom and knowledge of God! How unsearchable are his judgments and how inscrutable his ways!
>
> "For who has known the mind of the Lord,
>> or who has been his counselor?"
> "Or who has given a gift to him
>> that he might be repaid?"
>
> For from him and through him and to him are all things. To him be glory forever. Amen. (Rom. 11:33–36)

True peace and happiness come to the person who learns to say with all his heart, "It is the Lord. Let him do what seems good to him" (1 Sam. 3:18).

A person who persistently rejects the plain teaching of Scripture is not a believer—but it is also possible to believe many things that Scripture teaches and nevertheless be unconverted. True saving faith transforms those who have it. A faith without works is a dead, useless faith; it is the sort of faith that demons have. "You believe that God is one; you do well. Even the demons believe—and shudder!" (James 2:19). It is certainly possible to believe the Five Points of Calvinism and still be lost. I have known staunch Calvinists who have totally abandoned the Christian faith. I myself was a convinced Calvinist before I was converted. I remember debating Calvinistic doctrine with my classmates when I was in grade school and junior high school, and I was right—that is, my doctrine was right. I was wrong because I was in rebellion against God. I had submitted to the doctrine of the Scriptures, but I had not yet submitted to the Christ of the Scriptures.

Salvation is granted to those who receive a *person*—it is not promised to those who merely embrace a theological system, even if it is the right system. I am not, therefore, under the delusion that being a five-point Calvinist is an infallible certificate of Christian authenticity. I have known earnest, Christ-loving Christians who could not have told you what Calvinism was if their life depended on it. I believe the old farmer who sat across the table from me is an example.

It Encourages Missions and Evangelism

That leads me to another preliminary observation. Most people—even most Christians—do not know what Calvinism is. My farmer friend did not, and he still did not even after my two-sentence summary. Because most people do not know what Calvinism is, had he asked me point-blank, "Are you a Calvinist?" I would have said, "I honestly do not know what you are asking me. Could you please ask me what you want to know without using the word *Calvinist*?" That is not an evasive answer because, until he tells me, I do not know what the average person understands by the word *Calvinist*. Regrettably, if he has heard anything about Calvinism, it has probably been entirely negative and grossly misrepresented. I accurately anticipated the misinformation that my farmer friend had heard. He had heard that Calvinists do not believe in missions and evangelism. That is false, and it is perhaps the most widespread misconception about Calvinism. Since it is such a common misconception, I will address it briefly now and more fully later.

Some of the most ardent, zealous evangelists have been, and still are, Calvinists. Some of the greatest, most self-sacrificing missionaries throughout history and today were and are five-point Calvinists. The modern missions movement was commenced by William Carey, who spent his life ministering in India. He translated the Scriptures into multiple languages. He was a Calvinist. Adoniram Judson was the first American missionary. He labored for years in Burma before he saw his first convert. Now, two hundred years later, God has used his faithfulness to bring millions of people into Christ's kingdom. Judson was a Calvinist. David Brainerd was a missionary to the Native Americans in the 1700s. There was a great movement of God's Spirit among the Native Americans under Brainerd's ministry, and many were converted to follow Christ. Jonathan Edwards edited Brainerd's diary, and for many years God has used *The Life and Diary of David Brainerd* to lead countless other Christians to devote themselves to mission work. Brainerd was a Calvinist. And so was Edwards. George Whitefield, the mighty man of God whose preaching shook the world, was a Calvinist. C. H. Spurgeon, the Prince of Preachers, was an outspoken, ardent, five-point Calvinist.

In the face of such ample historical evidence, I am sometimes shocked to hear men who ought to know better make the unfounded assertion that Calvinism kills missions and evangelism. It might kill unbiblical, manipulative evangelistic methodologies, but it does not kill missions and evangelism. In fact, as I will attempt to make clear throughout this book, when properly understood, the Five Points of Calvinism ought to provide us with great motivation to be evangelistic, and they afford great encouragement to those who are evangelizing.

The Five Points teach that God has planned in advance for the success of the gospel, and this is greatly encouraging. It was encouraging to Jesus when he was surrounded by the hateful, disapproving faces of his countrymen who were rejecting him and plotting violence against him. When it appeared that all were rejecting him, he was surely comforted by the thought of God's sovereign plan when he said, "All that the Father gives me will come to me" (John 6:37). Jesus was encouraged knowing that his work would not be in vain.

God's sovereign choice of a people in Corinth was encouraging to the apostle Paul when the Jews of Corinth "opposed and reviled him" (Acts 18:6). He began preaching to the Gentiles in Corinth, and his life was in danger, but "the Lord said to Paul one night in a vision, 'Do not be afraid, but go on speaking and do not be silent, for I am with you, and no one will attack you to harm you, for I have many in this city who are my people" (Acts 18:9–10). Where is the encouragement here? Was the Lord assuring Paul by telling him that there were enough Christians in Corinth to protect him if a fight should erupt? No. The many in the city who Jesus described as *my people* were not yet converted, but they certainly would be. The Lord had planned for the success of the gospel in Corinth, and he was saying to Paul, "Be steadfast, immovable, always abounding in the work of the Lord, knowing that in the Lord your labor is not in vain" (1 Cor. 15:58). Paul was so encouraged by this vision from the Lord that "he stayed a year and six months, teaching the word of God among them" (Acts 18:11).

Some other common misunderstandings about Calvinism include the false assertion that Calvinists do not believe the Scripture "Whosoever will, let him take the water of life freely" (Rev. 22:17 KJV). We do. Others wrongly say that Calvinists believe that God will save people even if they do not want to be saved. We do not believe that. Others say that

Calvinists think that people will be saved without hearing and believing the gospel. We do not think that. There are numerous other misunderstandings and false accusations that demonstrate that the average person does not know much about Calvinism. I will discuss many of these misunderstandings in their proper place.

It Is a Worldview

Calvinism, then, is more than the Five Points. It is a way of looking at everything in the world. It is a way of thinking about everything. The Calvinistic way of thinking is rooted in the confidence that God is in control of everything and everyone and that he is controlling everything according to his good and perfect purpose. He does not force sinners to rebel against him, and he does not force saints to love and obey him; but all the while "he does according to his will among the host of heaven and among the inhabitants of the earth" (Dan. 4:35). Admittedly, this is a great mystery. All persons think and act freely, yet all the while God is sovereignly superintending all things so that his eternal purpose is infallibly accomplished. The Reverend William Jay asserted that "all parties act freely, yet necessarily too. . . . Ask me not for a solution. I only know the fact. I see the two ends of the chain, but the middle is under water; yet the connection is as real as it is invisible. By and by it will be drawn up."[3]

TULIP

In this book we will explore how God exercises his sovereign will in the salvation of sinners. That is the focus of the

---

3. William Jay, *Evening Exercises for Every Day in the Year* (repr., Harrisonburg, VA: Sprinkle Publications, 1999), 93.

Five Points. The Five Points may easily be remembered with the acrostic word *TULIP*. This mnemonic device helps us not only to remember the Five Points but also to remember them in their logical order.

T: *Total depravity.* This doctrine establishes the human need for divine grace.

U: *Unconditional election.* This shows that God the Father planned to save certain humans.

L: *Limited atonement.* This explains what God the Son did to accomplish God's plan.

I: *Irresistible grace.* This explains what God the Holy Spirit does to apply Christ's work to sinners.

P: *Perseverance of the saints.* This explains that sinners are permanently changed by God's work in them.

In each of the following chapters I will plainly describe the doctrine under consideration, examine the Bible to see whether the doctrine is taught there, answer the most common objections to it, and show how the doctrine ought to influence the way we think and live.

One final word: as noted above, TULIP presents the doctrines in their logical order. It is very helpful to read the following chapters in the order in which they appear. It is easier to understand and appreciate unconditional election if you have first understood what the Bible teaches about total depravity.

Questions for Contemplation and Discussion

1. Can you identify misunderstandings that you once had about Calvinism? What was the source of your misunderstanding?

2. If you once misunderstood Calvinism but are now a Calvinist, what changed your mind?

3. Have there been instances of your being falsely accused of believing something that you did not believe? Were you able to clear up the misunderstanding?

4. Both Calvinists and non-Calvinists tend to become angry when discussing Calvinistic doctrine. Why do you suppose this is the case?

5. What are some reasons why Calvinism has been so controversial? Which of these reasons are inevitable and which are avoidable?

6. What are some steps that Calvinists might take to make Calvinism less offensive to those who either are opposed to the doctrines or are hearing them for the first time?

7. Since Calvinism is so controversial, is it wise to simply keep quiet about it?

2

TOTAL DEPRAVITY

We Have Received a Bleak Diagnosis

Dead in Trespasses and Sins (Eph. 2:1)

Our Lord summarizes the doctrine of total depravity in one sentence: "No one can come to me unless the Father who sent me draws him" (John 6:44). Sin has so corrupted and disordered the human race that unless God intervenes in a person's life, he or she will never repent of sin and believe in the Lord Jesus Christ. Jesus is not asserting that every human is as bad as he might be; but according to Jesus, for reasons that we will explore, every human is unable to come to him unless the Father draws him or her. Since the primary issue is whether or not a person is able to come to Christ, perhaps it would be less confusing to call the doctrine *total inability*, but the common name is total depravity.

The *total* in *total depravity* does not mean that every human is as bad as he or she might possibly be; rather, it means that every component of human nature has been infected with sin. Stated another way, when we assert that every human is totally depraved, we are not saying that every human is totally *saturated* with sin. Rather, we are asserting that sin is totally *distributed* through every component of human nature.

For example, if we immersed a sponge into a bucket of vinegar, the sponge would soon be saturated with vinegar. That is, the sponge would be so full of vinegar it could not hold any more. If we removed the sponge and squeezed it out, no matter how hard we squeezed, every bit of the sponge would still be damp with the vinegar; and if we cut off any part of the sponge, it would still be damp and smell like vinegar. Similarly, while no human is completely saturated with sin, every component of human nature has been adversely affected by sin. If we separate and examine the various components of human nature (which I am about to do), every part is wet with sin and smells like sin.

Probably no one has ever been as wicked as is humanly possible. A murderer might love his mother, which is a good thing, and he might always have murdered one more person than he actually did, which would have made him worse. But a person who is not totally saturated with sin is nevertheless totally ruined by sin. A glass of water that contains only one drop of deadly poison is not as bad as one that contains ten drops, but it is still totally ruined by that one drop. Sin is a poison that pervades and ruins every component of human nature. The *total* in *total depravity*, then, refers to total distribution of sin and not to total saturation with sin.

What do I mean when I say that sin pervades and ruins every *component* of human nature? What are these components? When we talk about the nature of a thing or a person, we are talking about the essential qualities of that thing or person: the qualities or components that make that thing or person what it is. For example, a pie has two essential components. There is a crust, and there is a filling. There is the possibility of great variation in both the crust and the filling; but if you take away either the crust or the filling, you no longer have a pie. If we are to understand the doctrine of total depravity, we need to do a little thinking about the essential components of humans. I will identify these components, explore how God originally designed them to work, and point out how sin has adversely affected them. Then we will see why Jesus categorically states that no one can come to him unless the Father draws the person.

The Components: Understanding, Will, and Affections

When God created humans, he created us in his image so that we loved him and were capable of fellowship with him. He gave us the ability to understand the truth that he revealed. He made us so that we eagerly chose what was good. In this state of spiritual health, we loved God and loved all persons and things as God intended. In other words, he gave us enlightened understanding, free will, and healthy affections.[1] Stated another way, God created humans in knowledge, righteousness, and holiness.[2] These three qualities—understanding, will (sometimes called volition), and affections—are essential to what it means to be human, so we can say that these are the nonphysical components of human nature. When human

---

1. You may find a very helpful discussion of these three components in Calvin's *Institutes of the Christian Religion*, 1.15.3.

2. This is the language of the Westminster Shorter Catechism, answer 10, and the Baptist Catechism, answer 13. Late in the seventeenth century the Particular Baptists adopted the Shorter Catechism, revising the questions and answers having to do with baptism so that they reflected Baptist views. Other than those revisions, the Shorter Catechism and the Baptist Catechism are virtually identical.

nature is rightly ordered, it works like this: In submission to God, *understanding* is the ruler of the human soul, and the primary concern of the human is whether something is true. Then a healthy human will choose to believe the truth and order his life according to the truth. We want, or we *will*, to follow the truth. Volition obeys reason. We want to follow the truth because it appeals to us. We find it attractive. We love to do what is true and right. We are appropriately affected by the truth. *Affections* cooperate with understanding and volition so that we find pleasure in believing and obeying God.

In addition to these nonphysical components, God also gave us physical bodies with appetites and passions, and as long as these bodies with appetites and passions were subservient to man's higher purpose of knowing and enjoying God, all was well. This ideal, healthy state of human nature can be represented like this:

Understanding

Will

Affections

The Bible writers use the word *life* to refer to this ideal ordering of human nature. Before humans sinned, we had life and were happy. God was our ultimate source and standard of what was good and evil. In his love for humans, God gave us a reminder that our happy life depended on our continued obedience to him. That reminder was the Tree of the Knowledge of Good and Evil, and God told the humans not to eat the fruit of that tree, "for in the day that you eat of it you shall surely die" (Gen. 2:17).

Spiritual Death

We disobeyed God and ate the fruit (see Gen. 3:1–7), and God kept his word: the humans died. There was not some magic chemical in the fruit that caused death in the humans. Instead, the fruit of the Tree of the Knowledge of Good and Evil represented a way of thinking and living. As long as they left the fruit alone, the humans were submitting to an order of things in which God was their ultimate source of knowing what was good and evil. When they seized the fruit, however, they were saying, "Now we will determine for ourselves what is good and evil." God's threat came true at once. They lived physically for many years after eating the forbidden fruit, but the day they disobeyed God, they died spiritually. Human nature became corrupted and disordered. Human understanding was darkened, our affections were polluted, and our will became captivated by sin. Humans never lost understanding, volition, and affections, but all three components of human nature fell from their original condition of knowledge, righteousness, and holiness.

Not only that, but a couple of other devastating things happened. The understanding was dethroned from its place as the God-ordained ruler of man's soul, and affections began to rule. Humans' primary question was no longer "What does God say is true?" but became "What do I want?" Instead of following God-loving reason, the will began to follow sin-loving affection. Understanding was demoted to third place, where it was assigned the task of justifying the choices that we make. Human nature was turned upside down! The image of God was not obliterated in humans, but it was distorted. We still reflect his image, but we are like a broken mirror—the reflection is severely distorted.

In this diseased, disordered spiritual state, the concerns

of the body and of the physical world began to become unduly important to us. Humans began to live as if the only world that exists is the world that we experience through our physical senses. We began to live as if the world of the flesh were the only world there is. It can be represented like this:

This is spiritual death.

Sin, Death, the Natural Person, and the Flesh

In the Bible, the Holy Spirit uses several words to refer to this corrupt and disordered state of human nature. Sometimes he refers to it as being *in sin.* Sometimes he calls it *death.* Sometimes he calls it *the flesh,* and sometimes he calls it *the natural man.* He uses many other words too, but let us examine these four and think about their implications.

Sin

Sin is a word that means that something or someone is not where it is supposed to be; in one of its senses it means "missed the mark." If we were shooting arrows at a target, every arrow that missed the bull's-eye would have missed the mark. It would not be where we intended it to hit. God made humans to know him, love him, and be like him. You might say that God is the center of the bull's-eye for humans. The

Westminster Shorter Catechism asks, "What is the chief end of man?" The answer: "Man's chief end is to glorify God and to enjoy him forever."[3] Since the fall into sin, every human being who has ever lived (except our Lord) has failed to hit the mark and has instead lived in sin. In fact, from the moment we were conceived, we were in sin. "Behold, I was brought forth in iniquity, and in sin did my mother conceive me" (Ps. 51:5).

Death

The Holy Spirit also calls a person in this corrupt and disordered state *dead*.

> And you were dead in the trespasses and sins in which you once walked, following the course of this world, following the prince of the power of the air, the spirit that is now at work in the sons of disobedience. (Eph. 2:1–2)

This is a spiritual deadness—and remember that death is a fulfillment of the threat that was made to the first humans: "You shall surely die." As noted above, they did not die physically that very day, but they did die spiritually.

If, however, we think about what happens to a physical body that dies, we may gain some insight into the meaning of spiritual death. After all, when applied to humans' spiritual state, the word *death* is a metaphor, and metaphors are an effective way of communicating difficult ideas because they take something with which we are familiar and use it to teach us about something with which we are unfamiliar. What do we know about physical death? To say that someone is *dead* is the worst thing you can say about a person's physical

3. Westminster Shorter Catechism, question and answer 1.

condition. There is a vast difference between *critically ill* and *dead*. A physician might help you when you are critically ill, but only God can help you when you are dead.

There are two main consequences of physical death: first, the dead and the living no longer know one another, and second, the dead enter a state of decay.

The dead are separate from the living. When I say that the dead and the living no longer know one another, I am not saying that deceased persons know nothing about what is happening on earth—they may. However that may be, there is no doubt that a dead person is separated from fellowship with living persons. Dead persons do not know us the way they once did, and we no longer know them the way we once did. You may go to the grave of a dead loved one and pretend that you are talking to her, but she will not talk back. A separation has occurred.

In Bible language, when a person is in intimate relationship with another, he is said to *know* that person. For example, the Holy Spirit says that "Adam knew Eve his wife," and this is a delicate way of saying that he was intimately acquainted with her, for the consequence was that "she conceived and bore Cain" (Gen. 4:1). The Lord Jesus says that on the day of judgment he will say to imposters, "I never *knew* you; depart from me, you workers of lawlessness" (Matt. 7:23). Jesus knows all things, so he cannot be saying to them, "I was unaware of you." Instead, when he says "I never knew you," he is declaring that he and they had never been in close fellowship. They had not been friends.

In spiritual death, we no longer know God. We are no longer in intimate relationship with him. We can understand this about spiritual death by contrasting how Jesus describes someone who has eternal life: "This is eternal life, that they *know* you, the only true God, and Jesus Christ whom you have sent" (John 17:3). Though we were created capable of joyful fellowship with God, when we sin we are rebelling against God and his truth. We are saying, "I do not know you." God says we ought to love him above all else, and when we love other things more than him, he inevitably disapproves of our thinking and our actions. He is saying, "I do not know you."

The consequences of physical death picture what spiritual death is like. We are separated from the living God and no longer know him with the knowledge of loving relationship. We disagree with him about what is fundamentally important. He insists that loving him is the most essentially important purpose of human existence, and a spiritually dead person thinks it is something else. Even in human relationships we do not want to be friends with people who constantly disagree with our most fundamental and important beliefs. If such people go beyond mere disagreement and persistently condemn us for what we love, we outright avoid them when we can. As long as it is our nature to love sin, we will not want to know intimately a God who hates sin. We will persistently disagree with him about what is most important, and he will persistently disapprove of our sinful, self-destructive choices. No wonder Jesus says that no one can come to him unless the Father draws him. We do not *want* to go to Jesus.

In this dead condition it is impossible for us to do anything that pleases God, because no matter what it is, and no matter how much it may look like a good deed to us and to other humans, God will not be pleased with it. Why? Because we will do our alleged good deeds for some reason other than love of God.

Suppose I come home on my wedding anniversary with a bouquet of flowers for my wife. When I give them to her, she says, "Oh, thank you, Jim. They are beautiful."

I reply, "Now don't go getting all emotional. I only bought them because I knew you would be mad if I didn't get you anything. So take your stupid flowers and leave me alone."

Ought she to be pleased with such a loveless gift? Yet we act surprised when God is not pleased with our loveless efforts "to keep him happy." We are dead to him as long as we do not love him. We are separated from him like a dead person is separated from the living. "Your iniquities have made a separation between you and your God, and your sins have hidden his face from you so that he does not hear" (Isa. 59:2).

The dead enter a state of decay. Another consequence of physical death that affords us insight into the meaning of spiritual death is that after a person dies, he immediately begins to decay. The most beautiful woman in the world will not be physically beautiful after she dies. The strongest man in the world cannot even lift his little finger after he dies. What was once beautiful and strong becomes repulsive and powerless.

We know about the decay of dead bodies, but what happens to a person when he is dead spiritually? A physically dead body does not work at all, but it is not accurate to say that a spiritually dead person does nothing. He is active. We saw earlier that essential human nature consists of understanding, affections, and will. A spiritually dead person still has a functioning understanding, he has affections, and he has a will and freely chooses what he loves and thinks to be best.

Let us note how the Holy Spirit says that sin causes decay in these essential components of human nature. Consider Romans 3:10–12. (In brackets I will intersperse what is being said about human nature.)

None is righteous, no, not one; [*Considered singly, every human is wrong.*]

no one understands; [*The understanding is not working
right.*]
no one seeks for God. [*The will is misdirected.*]
All have turned aside; [*Made to love God, we turn aside to
pursue whatever it is that we prefer before God.
The affections are perverted.*] together they have
become worthless; [*Considered corporately, the
entire race is worthless when it comes to fulfilling
our original purpose.*]
no one does good,
not even one.

It is as if God says, "Let me take another look to make sure
that I have not overlooked someone who does good." After
making sure, he concludes, "No, not even one."

Consider Jesus's words recorded in John 3:19–20:

And this is the judgment: the light has come into the
world [*"light" is truth, which ought to be embraced by the
understanding*], and people loved the darkness [*the affections are perverted—we love the darkness of ignorance and
lies*] rather than the light because their works were evil
[*because we make life choices that are contrary to God's will,
our will is contrary to God's will*]. For everyone who does
wicked things hates the light [*this demonstrates perverted
affections and darkened understanding*] and does not come to
the light [*a person who does not choose the light has a corrupt
will*], lest his works should be exposed [*this all causes us to
say, "If God is going to make me leave the things I love, I'll just
stay away from God"*].

I was once witnessing to a friend, and he said to me,
"Jim, you don't understand; everything I love to do for fun is

sin. If I were to become a Christian, I would have to give up everything I love." Most people are not so forthright in admitting this, but it is, in fact, the case of all who refuse Christ. At the time, my friend probably supposed himself to be happy, but even if a person feels himself to be miserable in his sin, if left to himself he will not forsake his life of sin and run to the only one who can help him. "You were wearied with the length of your way, but you did not say, 'It is hopeless'" (Isa. 57:10). Though he may be weary *in* sin, he is not weary *of* sin, and he still hopes to find some way to continue in it. Should he once admit, "It is hopeless," there is hope for him.

Humans are filled with longings that can be satisfied only in God, and yet, because of the sinful decay of human nature, we are afraid of and averse to the God we so desperately need. An animal infected with rabies, or hydrophobia, is afraid of water. The animal must have water to survive, but, like a human infected with sin, it is repulsed by what it needs. Both rabies and sin induce a sort of madness. Those suffering from both disorders are out of their senses. Regarding those suffering the maddening influences of sin, the Holy Spirit says, "God may perhaps grant them repentance leading to a knowledge of the truth, and they may *come to their senses* and escape from the snare of the devil, after being captured by him to do his will" (2 Tim. 2:25–26).

The Natural Person

Our understanding is so badly decayed in spiritual death that we are no longer able to understand spiritual things. In fact, those spiritual things appear foolish to us. Consider 1 Corinthians 2:14: "The natural person does not accept the things of the Spirit of God, for they are folly to him, and he is not able to understand them because they are spiritually discerned." Notice that it is not *the notoriously wicked person* who does not accept the things of God; it is *the natural* person—the person in his natural state—the person whom God has left to his natural sin-deadened understanding, affections, and will. If God merely leaves a person alone, that person will never accept the things of the Spirit of God because, frankly, it all sounds foolish to him.

The Flesh

The natural person wants to live as if the natural world is the only world that really matters. Similarly, "those who live according to the flesh set their minds on the things of the flesh" (Rom. 8:5). In other words, such a person wants to live as if the world he can experience with his physical body, his flesh, is the only world there is. When a person rejects the spiritual in favor of the physical, he will not accept the things of God. He may continue to long for spiritual experiences because, in spite of all his efforts, he remains a spiritual being, but he will seek to fulfill his spiritual longings through physical means, such as sexual encounters and whatever physical things he puts in the place of God.

In fact, all sins are symptoms of a diseased, deadly way of thinking that humans have embraced. This deadly way of thinking may be compared to a sickness, similar to amnesia, that causes humans to forget why we were made and where our home is. Created to know God and to inhabit eternity, we live as if we were created only to enjoy the pleasures of earth and time. We have forgotten who we are. In our spiritual amnesia, we live as if we are not destined to inhabit eternity, and instead we live exclusively for temporary, earthly pleasures that we must leave behind when we die, if not sooner. Enjoying the pleasures of sense is a legitimate part of human experience, but we are to enjoy those pleasures in moderation, always remembering that we will leave them behind when we leave this world. Something that may be a blessing when it is enjoyed in moderation becomes a poison when it is enjoyed in excess or when it supplants our enjoyment of spiritual pleasures.

A person who is living according to the flesh may not be living a life of scandalous sin. He may just think about food all the time. She may just think about working out all the time. He might just love video games. She might love pop culture. Maybe they are hard-working, responsible citizens who just love to work in the yard, but if their minds are constantly occupied with the physical world of the flesh, they are dead.

> For to set the mind on the flesh is death, but to set the mind on the Spirit is life and peace. For the mind that is set on the flesh is hostile to God, for it does not submit to God's law; indeed, it cannot. Those who are in the flesh cannot please God. (Rom. 8:6–8)

Had you quoted this passage to me before I was converted and told me that my mind was hostile to God, I might have argued to the contrary, saying, "I admit that I may not love God, but I do not hate him. I just wish he would leave me alone. God would not be so bad if he were not against all the fun stuff I wish I could do. If he would help me get what I want, I might even like him." Never mind the fact that I sometimes wished that God never existed. I still would have protested, "But I do not hate him!" I daresay that if I had overheard someone expressing his wish that I had never existed, or if he observed that he found my whole personality repugnant, I might justly have concluded that the speaker was hostile toward me. Somehow I thought it was different when I felt that way toward God and his holy character. Is it any wonder that "those who are in the flesh cannot please

God"? We are hostile to God, and we really do not see the problem.

Since we remain spiritual beings and long for what God alone can supply, in our sinful state we sometimes fabricate a god who has a character that suits us in our sin. We may even call our god "Jesus." We want to remain in control of our lives and keep enjoying our sin, but we also want the benefits of having a god. Therefore we construct a god who approves of our sinful choices, and we delude ourselves into thinking that we are worshiping the true God. This allows us to dispense with whatever the Bible says about God. When we read something in the Bible that does not fit our conception of God, we dismiss it, saying, "My God is not like that. My God wants me to be happy." We go on living as if the natural world were the only world there is.

Someone might object, "But why must God take it so personally? All I am doing is living my life and minding my own business. Why can't God and I just leave each other alone?" God takes personally such an attitude from humans because he made humans to be in an intimate, loving relationship with him. I am not offended if the neighbor lady never kisses me when I come home from work. I never expected such a thing from her! If my wife, however, never kisses me, and if she does not want to be near me, I will take it personally. Why? We are married. I have legitimate expectations of her that I do not have of other women. The situation is similar with God and his expectations of us. He made us for himself. He provides for us and keeps us alive. He takes it personally when we refuse his light and prefer darkness. He takes it personally when we greedily snatch his physical gifts and then secretly wish he would go away.

Some time ago, a popular movie depicted a loving grandfather carefully crafting a handmade wooden dollhouse as a Christmas present for his granddaughter. It was plain that he put much effort and many hours into designing and building a gift that would express his love for his granddaughter. But on Christmas morning, the granddaughter threw a fit when she saw the dollhouse, protesting that she did not want an old wooden dollhouse; she wanted the plastic one she had seen in the toy store![4] Surely every viewer thought, *What a brat!*

> Be appalled, O heavens, at this;
>> be shocked, be utterly desolate,
>>> declares the LORD,
> for my people have committed two evils: .
> they have forsaken me,
>> the fountain of living waters,
> and hewed out cisterns for themselves,
>> broken cisterns that can hold no water. (Jer. 2:12–13)

We do not want the fountain of living waters; we want the leaky, store-bought, plastic wading pools of earthly pleasures. The angels must think, *What a bunch of brats!*

It ought to be growing clearer why Jesus asserts that no one can come to him unless the Father draws him. Why would a sin-loving person ever freely choose to submit to a sin-killing Christ who was sent to reconcile him to a God

---

4. See "The Watch Pig," *Babe*, directed by Chris Noonan (1995; Universal City, CA: Universal Studios Home Entertainment, 2003), DVD. In this charming little movie, some of the humans demonstrate an unworthy, animal-like character, while the animals demonstrate admirable, human-like character. The animals come out looking better than many of the humans. God makes a similar point when he says, "The ox knows its owner, and the donkey its master's crib, but Israel does not know, my people do not understand" (Isa. 1:3).

whom he does not like, and who would ultimately take him to a place where he would be in the presence of God forever with a bunch of people who think something is wise that he thinks is foolish—a place where he will never again be able to enjoy the sins that he loves?

Such a person *cannot* come to Christ because he *will not* come to Christ; he does not want to come. In his understanding he thinks spiritual things are foolish. In his affections he loves darkness rather than light. He has so persistently chosen to follow his own way that "the iniquities of the wicked ensnare him, and he is held fast in the cords of his sin" (Prov. 5:22). His ears are so full of the devil's lies that he can no longer hear God's voice.

> Behold, their ears are uncircumcised,
>> they cannot listen;
> behold, the word of the LORD is to them an object of scorn;
>> they take no pleasure in it. (Jer. 6:10)

> Their deeds do not permit them
>> to return to their God.
> For the spirit of whoredom is within them,
>> and they know not the LORD. (Hos. 5:4)

Dead in trespasses and in sins, he has only one hope: the resurrecting power of God. What he needs "depends not on human will or exertion, but on God, who has mercy" (Rom. 9:16). He must be born from above or he will never even see the kingdom of God, much less enter it (see John 3:3, 5). He must be "born, not of blood nor of the will of the flesh nor of the will of man, but of God" (John 1:13).

Answering Objections

If no one is able to come to Jesus unless the Father draws him, then why does God command everyone to believe on Jesus? Why command what is impossible? When God commands us to do something, shouldn't we assume that we can obey his command? Is God sincere?

The Offer of Salvation to All Is a Sincere Offer

God is sincere when he offers salvation to all who repent and believe. It is true that whosoever will may come to Jesus. Beyond merely permitting us, God commands us to believe in Jesus! "And this is his commandment, that we believe in the name of his Son Jesus Christ" (1 John 3:23). Left to ourselves, however, we will never obey him and come to Christ. He freely offers life to all in Christ, but the freeness and sincerity of the invitation demonstrate the obstinacy and depravity of those who refuse it.

Refusal of the Sincere Offer Confirms God's Justice in Condemning Sinners

When humans reject God's gracious offer of forgiveness through Christ, that refusal makes it obvious that God is just when he condemns the unrepentant. Nearly all my students are diligent and conscientious in applying themselves to the assignments I give them in my classes. Very few students fail, but it occasionally happens, and it is not uncommon for a failing student to ask for some extra work in order to bring his grade up to passing. If that student has turned in all his assignments, then I might give him some extra work. If the student does not do the extra work, then it becomes obvious that he deserved to fail. When God first made humans, he put them to the test. We failed the test. Now God has provided a way for us to have our sins forgiven and be reconciled to him. He has sent his only Son to be our Savior. If we reject his offer of grace through Jesus, it becomes obvious that we deserve to fail and to suffer God's condemnation.

Human Inability Is the Result of Human Disobedience

Remember Jesus's words, "The light has come into the world, and people loved the darkness rather than the light because their works were evil" (John 3:19). Men have deliberately chosen to do evil deeds, and there are far-reaching consequences to this. Namely, they love darkness and refuse the light. Ought God now to say, "Well, since you love darkness so much, I will revise my expectations of humans and will no longer require you to come to the light"?

Suppose a thief appears before a judge and says, "Judge, if you let me out of jail, I will just steal again—because, the fact is, I love to steal. You might say I'm addicted to stealing. I don't even need all the stuff I steal; I just love the thrill of stealing. I enjoy getting to use stuff that I have not paid for, and frankly, I do not care how hard someone else has worked for something he owns—when I want it, I steal it. There is no point in your telling me to get a job and pay for stuff. I am not going to obey you." Ought the judge to say, "I see your point. Therefore I will not tell you to get a job and become a law-abiding citizen"?[5] Of course not. The law remains the same. God's law remains the same even though sinners are so in love with sin that they have no intention of repenting. Remember—men *cannot* come because they *will* not. Sin has debilitating, enslaving effects.

---

5. This is my own version of an illustration suggested in at least one sermon by C. H. Spurgeon. See his "Human Inability" in Charles H. Spurgeon, *New Park Street Pulpit* (London, 1859; repr., Pasadena, TX: Pilgrim Publications, 1981), 4:141.

Everyone who practices sin is a slave to sin. (John 8:34)

Do you not know that if you present yourselves to anyone as obedient slaves, you are slaves to the one whom you
obey, either of sin, which leads to death, or of obedience,
which leads to righteousness? (Rom. 6:16)

Through prolonged exposure to pornography, a man
can develop such perverted views of women that he becomes
incapable of normal healthy relations with his wife. Through
prolonged indulgence in sinful thinking, a person becomes
incapable of hearing and obeying God. Is the wife, or is God,
supposed to abandon the desire and expectation for what
ought to be normal, healthy relationships and accommodate
to a sinful, new normal instead?

An illustration. Human inability is the result of human disobedience. Suppose a man says to his sons one morning, "Boys,
I want you to be sure to mow the grass today. Also, I poured
a section of concrete in the sidewalk early this morning, and
the cement is still wet. Stay out of it. And one more thing:
your mother has told me that you boys are wearing your
headphones all day, and this makes it impossible for her to
get your attention when she needs you, so do not wear your
headphones today. I'll be back this afternoon."

Later that afternoon when the father returns, the grass
has not been mowed, and he sees his sons standing in the
fresh concrete, which has hardened around their feet. They
are wearing their headphones. His wife meets him at the
door, and she says, "I have not been able to get those boys to
do a thing today. They will not answer me when I call." He
goes outside to where the boys are standing in the concrete
and motions for them to take off their headphones. They take

them off, and he says to them, "Boys, I thought I told you to mow the grass today."

They answer, "Dad, we could not do it. We're stuck in this concrete, which has hardened around our feet, and we can't move."

Their dad says, "And your mother tells me that she has been calling you and that you haven't answered her."

They answer, "Dad, we have not heard her. Honest! We have been listening to our headphones all day."

Their inability to obey and their inability to hear are a result of their disobedience.[6] There is one notable way that the disobedient boys in this illustration differ from the disobedient sinners who cannot hear God. In the illustration, as a result of their disobedience, the boys are physically (or naturally) unable to obey and hear their parents. In the case of sinners, disobedience has led not to a *natural* inability but to a *moral* inability to obey and hear God. All the essential components of human nature are still intact in a rebellious sinner, but their rebellious ideas, their perverted desires, and their sinful choices render them unable to come to Christ.

We must learn our inability. One final thought on this question of why God commands sinners to come to Jesus when they cannot do so without his aid: learning that we cannot save ourselves is an indispensable first step in our salvation. For example, keeping God's law was never intended to be a way of salvation. One of the main reasons that he gave his law is to make people give up on the idea of earning salvation by doing good works.

---

6. This is an expansion of an illustration that I heard from the late Edward Overbey, who taught for many years at Lexington Baptist College in Lexington, Kentucky.

Now we know that whatever the law says it speaks to those who are under the law, so that every mouth may be stopped, and the whole world may be held accountable to God. For by works of the law no human being will be justified in his sight, since through the law comes the knowledge of sin. (Rom. 3:19–20)

Now the law came in to increase the trespass. (Rom. 5:20)

When God gives us commands that we cannot keep perfectly, at least part of the reason is so that we will realize our inability and look to him for help. As long as we think we are well, we will not go to the doctor.

Effects

If you are not a devoted follower of Jesus Christ, the doctrine of total depravity ought to make you see just how desperate your condition is. Perhaps you have lived under the delusion that you will enjoy living in sin until you are ready to get right with the Lord, and then you will take care of things quickly and easily. After all, how hard can it be to "just believe"? Anyone who thinks that exercising faith is an easy matter has probably not made any significant efforts toward attempting it. "Can the Ethiopian change his skin or the leopard his spots? Then also you can do good who are accustomed to do evil" (Jer. 13:23). Your case is dire. God requires you to do something that you cannot do unless he draws you. You cannot make yourself believe what you think to be foolish. You cannot make yourself love light when you love darkness. You must be born again, but you cannot give birth to yourself.

Perhaps you have fancied that "it's all up to you," and you have believed the lie that you are the master of your fate. Now you ought to be realizing that your only hope for a happy life on earth and in eternity lies in the hands of the God whom you have hated and against whom you have rebelled. What should you do?

Seek the Lord

> Seek the LORD while he may be found;
>   call upon him while he is near;
> let the wicked forsake his way,
>   and the unrighteous man his thoughts;
> let him return to the LORD, that he may have compassion
>   on him,
>   and to our God, for he will abundantly pardon. (Isa.
>   55:6–7)

Whoever believes on Jesus "will not perish but have eternal life" (John 3:16). If you are going to believe on Jesus, you must know something about him. Read the Bible. Start with the gospel of John. That book was written "so that you may believe that Jesus is the Christ, the Son of God, and that by believing you may have life in his name" (John 20:31). Go to a church where the Bible is believed and preached, and listen to the Word of God. "Faith comes from hearing, and hearing through the word of Christ" (Rom. 10:17). Read the rest of this book! The Five Points of Calvinism are a summary of what the Bible teaches about what God has done to save sinners.

Praise God for His Grace

If you already are a devoted follower of Christ, you know that you are a sinner saved by God's grace, but perhaps you have never before realized just how much grace God bestowed on you. Our appreciation for grace is tied to our understanding of sin. If we think that our sin is little, we will love little. When we see our sin to be deep, we see God's grace to be high. When we gain fresh insight into our awful sin, we ought to respond with fresh praises for God's amazing grace.

Adjust Your View of Evangelism

When we understand the doctrine of total depravity, not only should it make us depend on God's power for our own salvation, but it should also make us feel how dependent we are on God's divine power in our efforts to bring others to Christ. When we understand that sinners are dead in trespasses and in sin, then manipulative psychological techniques parading as evangelistic methodologies appear as they are: cheap, tawdry tricks. "We have renounced disgraceful, underhanded ways. We refuse to practice cunning or to tamper with God's word, but by the open statement of the truth we would commend ourselves to everyone's conscience in the sight of God" (2 Cor. 4:2). In our evangelistic endeavors, anything less than the power of God that raised Jesus from the dead is useless. It does no good to put a bandage on a dead man.

Imagine that a friend has asked you to go visit an unconverted man in order to share the gospel with him. You agree and drive to the address that he gives you. The house is a mansion set in the wealthiest neighborhood in town. Your anxiety begins to rise as you remember "how difficult it is for those who have wealth to enter the kingdom of God" (Luke 18:24).

You ring the bell. A butler answers and says that Mr. _____ will receive you in the library. He lets you into the library and announces your arrival to a man who is seated with his back to the door. You cannot help but notice that the library is massive. Your anxiety increases as you realize that he is not only rich but is also an intellectual. You recall the Bible's words that "not many of you were wise according to worldly standards" (1 Cor. 1:26).

The butler closes the door behind you, and you are left alone in this cavernous room with a person who has not spoken and has not even made the effort to turn around to look at you. Your steps echo on the polished marble floor as you walk toward the still silent and motionless figure. You think, *How rude. Why did I agree to make this visit?* You stop behind his chair and introduce yourself, but he does not move. You walk around to where you can see his face, and upon seeing him, you gasp as you realize why he has been so unresponsive: his face is blue. He is dead. It is worse than you thought.

Yes, sinners are dead. Cleverness and psychological techniques are useless. All you and I can do is speak the truth and pray and love, but we cannot raise the dead. God raises the dead. He must do it. You and I cannot. It is a good day when we learn to do God's work in God's place, using God's methods, at God's pace.

"You Can't Tell Me What to Do!"

We have seen that sin has ruined human nature. Each part of human nature has been ruined: The understanding does not accept God's truth. The affections love sin. The will persistently and without exception chooses a course that leads away from God. Not only is every part of human nature ruined, but the various components are even disarranged—turned upside down.

Sinful human nature may be compared to a house that has been decimated by a tornado. All the parts of the house still exist, but they have all been damaged in the tornado. All the pieces may be there, but they are scattered all over the yard. The Lord looked one day at the mess that humans had become, and "the LORD saw that the wickedness of man was great in the earth, and that every intention of the thoughts of his heart was only evil continually" (Gen. 6:5). Ask yourself, "How could such a thoroughly ruined and depraved person suddenly decide one day that he wanted to do something that no part of him is attracted to doing?" His understanding does not think that Jesus is a good idea. He loves sin and not a sin-hating Lord. He chooses to sin as much as he dares to. Which part of him wants to come to Jesus?

As noted early in this chapter, *total depravity* could be more accurately called *total inability*. We are coming close to understanding total inability when we think of it as total indisposition—but total indisposition toward God is not the whole of the doctrine. We come still closer when we understand that our natural indisposition toward God is owing to our total disposition toward a way of thinking that is opposed to God and his ways. That is, in our sin we are not neutral; we are part of the rebel forces opposed to God. We are part of a cosmic spiritual rebellion led by Satan. Jesus said, "Why do you not understand what I say? It is because you cannot bear to hear my word. You are of your father the devil, and your will is to do your father's desires" (John 8:43–44). This explains why even a good thing like God's holy law provokes us to sin more.

Imagine two cups of liquid: one water, the other vinegar. I drop a teaspoon of baking soda into the water, and it sinks to the bottom. I drop a teaspoon of the soda into the vinegar, and it foments and foams. If I were watching someone perform this experiment from another room, I could immediately tell which cup contained the vinegar because it is the nature of vinegar to react violently to soda. The case is similar when God's command comes to a rebel. "But sin, seizing the opportunity afforded by the commandment, produced in me every kind of covetous desire . . . When the commandment came, sin sprang to life" (Rom. 7:8–9 NIV). Why? Because sin is essentially rebellion, and rebellion resents authority. The commandment is based in God's authority. The rebel says, "You can't tell me what to do." Totally depraved, the sinner reacts rebelliously against God's commandments by his very nature—including the commandment to repent and believe the gospel.

Our Only Hope

Once we understand what the Bible teaches about human inability, we see that if God does not intervene, no one will come to Christ and be saved from sin. God does intervene, and he intervenes according to a plan that he made before he created the world. In eternity past, he determined that he would love and save certain persons, called the elect, and that he would provide all the means for their salvation. He chose these persons to be his own people whom he would give to Christ. He sent Jesus to die in order to pay for the sins of these elect. He sends the Holy Spirit to persuade and enable the elect to embrace Jesus Christ as he is freely offered to us in the gospel. After doing so much to mend the broken relationship with his elect, he adopts them into his family and transforms them into sons and daughters who love him. We know him again. He commences the process of restoring and repairing our broken, disordered nature.

As a result of his grace, we are governed once again by God-informed reason. We come to our senses. He purifies our affections, and we become lovers of God. He renews our wills, and we freely choose to come to Christ and embrace him as our prophet, our priest, and our king. All these blessings flow from a gracious, loving God who determined that he would not leave all mankind to perish in the state of sin and misery. Out of his mere good pleasure, he elected some to everlasting life and entered into a covenant of grace in order to deliver them out of the state of sin and misery and to bring them into a state of salvation by a Redeemer.[7] That gracious election is the subject of the following chapter.

Questions for Contemplation and Discussion

1. Second Timothy 2:26 describes conversion as a person *coming to his or her senses*. What evidence can you identify in your own life that, before coming to Christ, you were out of your senses?

2. Since unconverted persons are often very intelligent, it is not a lack of intellectual capacity that hinders them from understanding the truth and embracing Christ. What are some of the reasons they are unable to come to Christ on their own?

3. Many believe that God's judgment against sinners—eternal damnation in hell—seems unnecessarily harsh. Reflecting on what you have learned in this chapter, how might you explain the justice of hell? What makes sin so bad that God sends sinners to hell?

4. Can an unconverted person do good works? Explain.

5. Saint Augustine famously wrote, "Our hearts are restless until they find rest in you." Similarly, Boethius, an influential Christian of the sixth century, wrote that humans inevitably seek for happiness and that happiness can be found only in God. The Bible states that no one seeks God. Can you harmonize Augustine and Boethius with what the Bible says?

7. Many of the ideas and phrases in this paragraph are taken from the Westminster Shorter Catechism (see questions 18–21, 23–26, and 31).

6. Before you came to Christ, how did you justify the sinful life you lived and the sinful choices you made? What were some of the lies you believed? What assisted you in maintaining your self-deception?
7. In one sentence, can you summarize the doctrine of Total Depravity?

UNCONDITIONAL ELECTION

The Father Planned for the Success of the Gospel

"He Chose Us in Him" (Eph. 1:4)

It was a Sunday evening, and I was preaching in a lovely antebellum church building in rural Kentucky. My text for the sermon was 2 Peter 1:5–11, which includes the exhortation to "make your calling and election sure" (v. 10 KJV). The congregation was small—maybe twenty people—and the setting was informal. When I came to verse 10, I said very little about election. As I recall, I said something like, "Election can be controversial, but you see that it is here in my text. Some form of the word *election* or *predestination* appears around fifty times in the New Testament, so you must believe something about the doctrine of election. If you believe the Bible, you have got to believe in election." I said little else about election, and I went on with the rest of the sermon. Election was not the main point of the text, so I never made it the main point of my sermon.

At the conclusion of the sermon, I dismissed the congregation, and everyone began the quiet, friendly conversations that inevitably arise in a loving church where people have known one another for years. Several people got up and began to mill about, mostly just to stretch their legs. No one was in a hurry to leave.

Suddenly, in a voice that could be heard above the chatter, an older gentleman called out, "What benefit is it for me to believe the doctrine of election?"

Everyone got quiet, returned to his or her seat, and looked at me expectantly. I said, "That is a good question. Open your Bibles to Romans 9."

For about the next thirty minutes, I explained the doctrine of unconditional election from Romans 9, emphasizing what is said in that chapter about the benefits of believing the doctrine. (I intend to do the same thing later in this chapter.) In the course of the dialogue that took place that evening, a brother prefaced his question by stating, "Now, I do not believe in election, but . . ."

We were on friendly terms, and we were not quarrelling, so I interrupted him and cheerfully reminded him of what I had just said in the sermon: "You have got to believe something about election. You cannot say that you don't believe in election, because it is in the Bible."

Unconditional Election Defined

Many people recognize that election is in the Bible, and they do believe something about election, but they do not believe in *unconditional* election that guarantees the salvation of the elect. I am about to examine a couple of those alternatives to unconditional election; but first let me define as clearly as I can what I mean when I write about unconditional election.

The Bible teaches that before God had created anyone or anything, he decided that he would choose, or *elect*, some humans to be his adopted children. No one deserved this honor; God did not foresee any *condition* in them that prompted him to choose them, so we say that God chose them *unconditionally*. God chose or elected them because he wanted to; or, to put it another way, it was his will to elect them.

Since his chosen people, along with the rest of mankind, would fall into sin, God planned to save them from their sin, and he also planned or *predestined* all the means to bring about their salvation. He planned that Christ would redeem his chosen ones; he planned that the Holy Spirit would enlighten and enliven his chosen ones and call them to Christ; and he planned all the providential arrangements to make sure that each of his chosen ones would hear the gospel and receive Christ as Lord. God the Father gave this group of chosen ones, the *elect*, as a gift to Christ to be his people, his sheep, and his bride. All of God's elect will be saved, and they are the only humans who will be saved.

Alternative 1: Universal Election

I once heard a preacher say that all the confusion caused by the doctrine of election was unnecessary, and that he was going to clear up the matter in only three sentences. He then said, "God casts one vote for you. Satan casts a vote against you. You cast the deciding vote." The preacher was asserting that God chose everyone. This would be universal election.

If God chose everyone to be saved, then election is virtually meaningless because it does not accomplish anything. If

universal election merely makes salvation possible for everyone, then it does not guarantee the salvation of anyone, and
we have to admit that it has been mostly ineffective. The overwhelming majority of persons who have ever lived have not
gone to heaven, "for the gate is narrow and the way is hard
that leads to life, and those who find it are few" (Matt 7:14).
If God's choosing a person indicates that he intends for that
person to be saved, then either God is unable to carry out his
intentions or else he must not be very skilled at arranging circumstances. Most humans live and die in circumstances that
are devoid of gospel witness. While this is true even today,
before the gospel was sent to the Gentiles, vast multitudes—
entire cultures—perished "separated from Christ, alienated
from the commonwealth of Israel and strangers to the covenant of promise, having no hope and without God in the
world" (Eph. 2:12). In those dark days, God had sovereignly
chosen to reveal himself to only one nation: Israel.

I find it remarkable that even those Christians who reject
unconditional election seem undisturbed by the fact that God
chose only Israel to be his chosen people. Their protest against
unconditional election unto salvation is that it is not fair to the
non-elect. They say, "That means that some people never get
the opportunity to be saved." It is correct that some people
never get the opportunity to be saved, but did we really need
the doctrine of election to bring this fact to our attention? Our
own observation can teach us this. A person must believe the
gospel in order to be saved. Before he can believe, he must
hear the gospel. Those who do not hear have no hope of being
saved. God is in control of when and where people are born.
He planned for you to be born in a place and time such that
you would hear the gospel. The same day that you were born,
thousands of other people were born who might never hear
the name of Jesus one time in their entire lives. Is this fair?

Not only our observation, but also an unbiased reading of Scripture, makes it plain that God has not given all peoples an equal opportunity to know him. Throughout the Bible, we read of how God favored Israel. He said to Israel, "The LORD your God has chosen you to be a people for his treasured possession, out of all the peoples who are on the face of the earth" (Deut. 7:6). Israel did nothing to deserve God's special notice. In the succeeding verses, the Lord explains why he chose Israel: "It was not because you were more in number than any other people that the LORD set his love on you and chose you, for you were the fewest of all peoples, but it is because the LORD loves you and is keeping the oath that he swore to your fathers" (vv. 7–8). Note the reasoning of this passage: "Why did the Lord choose you? Because he loved you. Why did the Lord love you? Because he loves you." There was simply no condition in Israel that attracted God to choose them. Is this fair?

Perhaps God's election of Israel does not bother most Christians because they fail to realize that in choosing to shed his light in Israel, God was leaving the rest of the world to perish in darkness. Just a few minutes of consideration ought to reveal that if God chose Israel and did not choose the rest of the world, this violates the principle by which many determine fairness: namely, that fairness means equal treatment of all concerned.

We need to revise our understanding of what constitutes fairness. Fairness does not consist in treating everyone equally; fairness consists in giving everyone what he deserves. Based on what we learned in the previous chapter on Total Depravity, surely we do not want God to treat us fairly. We do not want to get what we deserve. We cannot read far in the Bible before we are confronted with the reality that God does not treat all persons equally. One of the fundamental principles of Scripture is that God is not obligated to show mercy to anyone. And if he is not obligated to show mercy to anyone, then he cannot be unfair if he shows mercy to no one. How then is it unfair if he shows mercy to only one person, or to only one nation, or to as many as he chooses?

I suspect that many of those who assert that God has chosen everyone to be saved are trying to protect God from accusations of being unfair. Others may be trying to avoid a teaching that appears inevitably to lead to fatalism. I will address this concern later in this chapter. Whatever the case, if God has chosen everyone, then election is essentially meaningless since it accomplishes nothing. When we take into account the implications of God's exclusive favor toward Israel, we cannot conclude that God chose everyone.

Alternative 2: Conditional Election

Those who hold to conditional election may acknowledge that before creation God chose certain persons to be saved, and that he did not elect everyone, but according to their view God chose his elect because, knowing everything, he foresaw that they would repent of sin and put their faith in Christ. When he saw that these persons would repent and believe, he chose them. Repentance and faith are the conditions that prompted God to choose the elect, so that is why it is conditional election.

In order for this to be a fair and unbiased election, God waited to see what people would do before he elected any to be saved. To be consistent, God could not make any special arrangements that would make it more likely that anyone would repent and believe—that would be interfering with man's free will. After all, someone as intelligent and powerful as God can easily manipulate a person's decision-making process, and that would be unfair.

This view is sometimes presented as the Tunnel of Time theory: God looked down through the tunnel of time and saw who would believe, and he chose them, but his choosing them did not influence them to believe. They did that on their own. Unconditional election presents us with a God who plans; conditional election presents us with a God who reacts.

There are several significant problems with the doctrine of conditional election, and I will point out some of them once I begin explaining unconditional election, but I will mention two here.

First, based on what we learned in the chapter on Total Depravity, if left to ourselves, no one will ever repent of sin and believe in Christ.

> None is righteous, no, not one;
>> no one understands;
>> no one seeks for God.
> All have turned aside; together they have become worth-
>> less;
>> no one does good,
>> not even one. (Rom. 3:10–12)

In this passage from Romans 3, it is almost as if the Holy Spirit anticipates the Tunnel of Time theory and says, "God DID look down through the tunnel of time searching for anyone who was righteous, or anyone who would do good, or anyone who would seek for God. He double-checked the tunnel. How many did he find? Not even one."

A second problem with conditional election is an inconsistency found in those who hold to it. As I have already pointed out, those who believe in conditional election often hold this position because it seems unfair that God would choose his elect for no apparent reason. In their minds, in order for election to be fair it must be because God chooses to save those who on their own—without any divine intervention—repent and believe. Here is the problem: virtually no one prays in a way that is consistent with that view. No one prays, "Father, I want my loved ones to be saved, but I know that you respect everyone's free will, and you have already done all that you can legitimately do while still being a God of fairness. So be sure to leave my lost loved ones to themselves, and do not influence their thinking about sin or about Christ. Do not arrange providential circumstances so that you influence them to be sick of sin and to long for you. I know that you are a gentleman, so hold your powers of influence in reserve and let them decide for themselves." No! We do not want God to leave them alone. We want God to intervene. But if God intervenes, then he has influenced a person to repent and believe, and therefore, when he looked down through the tunnel of time and saw this person's repentance and faith, it was a repentance and faith that came about because he influenced the person. Not fair.

The Bible teaches us that God chose certain persons to be saved and that he did not choose everyone. Neither did he choose his elect because he foresaw that they would choose him first. Through the Great Rebellion, all mankind was plunged into a state of sin and misery, but God did not leave all mankind to perish in this state of sin and misery that we brought upon ourselves. God, having out of his mere good pleasure from all eternity elected some to everlasting life, entered into a covenant of grace in order to deliver his elect out of the state of sin and misery and to bring them into a state of salvation by a Redeemer.[1]

---

1. See the Westminster Shorter Catechism, question and answer 20.

Two Powerful Texts

In this chapter, even though I am not giving an exposition of a book of the Bible, I am going to explain two texts that emphasize the doctrine of unconditional election. I do not intend to give a thorough explanation of these passages, but I will focus on what they say about unconditional election.

Ephesians 1:3–14

> Blessed be the God and Father of our Lord Jesus Christ, who has blessed us in Christ with every spiritual blessing in the heavenly places, even as he chose us in him before the foundation of the world, that we should be holy and blameless before him. (vv. 3–4)

Note first the pervasive influence of election. Every spiritual blessing is here connected to God's having chosen us in Christ. Election is not merely some optional garnish on the main dish; election is the process God used to plan the meal.

Also, notice when God chose us: "before the foundation of the world." This strongly intimates that his choosing was not based on something we had done or on anything that he in his omniscience foresaw that we would do. In other words, he chose us unconditionally. He did not choose us because we were already holy and blameless, or because he foresaw that we had the initial graces of faith and repentance that come at the beginning of a life of holiness. He chose us that we should be holy and blameless.

The great goal for the elect is that we might be holy and blameless. The elect are changed into holy men and women. When we see the evidences of God's sanctifying grace in our lives, we make our calling and election sure (see 2 Peter 1:10).

> In love he predestined us for adoption to himself as sons through Jesus Christ, according to the purpose of his will, to the praise of his glorious grace, with which he has blessed us in the Beloved. (Eph. 1:4–6)

Not only did God choose us to be holy and blameless, he also predestined us for adoption. This makes it doubly clear that election is unto salvation and that we are not merely elected to opportunity or service. This verse excludes the possibility of universal election unless you are willing to take the even more unbiblical step of asserting universal salvation. Those whom God chooses become sons.

> For those whom he foreknew he also predestined to be conformed to the image of his Son, in order that he might be the firstborn among many brothers. And those whom he predestined he also called, and those whom he called he also justified, and those whom he justified he also glorified. (Rom. 8:29–30)

What is the motivation for such lavish grace? God did this because he wanted to do it this way—"according to the purpose of his will" (Eph. 1:5). Every Christian prays that God's will may be done, and we rejoice when it is done. Jesus once declared, "I thank you, Father, Lord of heaven and earth, that you have hidden these things from the wise and understanding and revealed them to little children; yes, Father, for such was your gracious will" (Matt. 11:25–26). The doctrine of election helps us direct our praise to the one to whom it is due—to God, for the praise of his glorious grace. God must get all the glory for our salvation, and not one bit of the credit can go to us or to any other human.

We did not choose him because we were more spiritually

minded than someone else. We did not choose him because we were intelligent enough to see that it was the right thing to do. We were part of the world that "did not know God through wisdom" (1 Cor. 1:21). Jesus said, "You did not choose me, but I chose you" (John 15:16). The doctrine of unconditional election ought to cultivate the deepest humiliation in us and provoke the highest praise from us.

The channel of this grace is Christ, for we have these blessings in the Beloved. The blessings of election are not promised or conferred apart from Christ, his work, and his gospel.

Some, hearing of the doctrine of election, protest that it is nothing more than fatalism. They say, "If God has already decided who is going to be saved, then why preach? Why send missionaries? Why pray?" Our text in Ephesians 1 gives the answer that we do these things because God has predestined that all his elect receive every spiritual blessing in Christ (see v. 3), that they be adopted as sons through Jesus Christ (see v. 5), and that they are blessed in the Beloved (see v. 6). The elect do not go to heaven merely because God chose them; Christ qualifies us for heaven. God not only predestined our salvation but also predestined the means of our salvation— the work that Christ would do on our behalf, the work of the Holy Spirit in us, and our faith in him.

Note how these various means are specified in the passage under consideration: redemption through the blood of Christ (see v. 7), the forgiveness of sins (see v. 7), the revelation of the mystery of his will (see v. 9), hope in Christ (see v. 12), and belief in him (see v. 13). Consequently, we do not believe that the elect will be saved apart from the means that God has appointed. Rather, God uses his appointed means to save his elect.

Note finally from this text that the sovereignty of God

over all things makes it certain that election will result in salvation for the elect. In him we have obtained an inheritance, having been predestined according to the purpose of him who works all things according to the counsel of his will (see v. 11). God arranges all circumstances so that his elect hear the gospel, believe the gospel, and receive all that is necessary to obtain the inheritance.

Romans 9:6–23

Before coming to the material contained in Romans 9, the Holy Spirit has already explained that both Jews and Gentiles are saved the same way: entirely by grace through faith. In Romans 9, the Spirit points out that this is not a new arrangement.

No Jew was ever saved merely because he was a descendent of Abraham. "For not all who are descended from Israel belong to Israel, and not all are children of Abraham because they are his offspring, but 'Through Isaac shall your offspring be named'" (vv. 6–7). From the family of Abraham, God chose some, but not all, to be his children. "This means that it is not the children of the flesh who are the children of God, but the children of the promise are counted as offspring" (v. 8). Abraham was the father of Ishmael as well as Isaac, but God chose Isaac and not Ishmael to be the recipient of the promise. "For this is what the promise said: 'About this time next year I will return, and Sarah shall have a son'" (v. 9).

But God was not finished electing from the family; after choosing only one of Abraham's sons, Isaac, he then chooses only one of Isaac's twin sons, Jacob—but not Esau.

> And not only so, but also when Rebekah had conceived children by one man, our forefather Isaac, though they were not yet born and had done nothing either good or bad—in

order that God's purpose of election might continue, not because of works but because of him who calls—she was told, "The older will serve the younger." As it is written, "Jacob I loved, but Esau I hated." (vv. 10–13)

Notice several things here.

- Having godly parents does not guarantee that a person will be one of God's elect.
- The election of Jacob instead of Esau was unconditional. They "were not yet born and had done nothing either good or bad."
- One of God's purposes in election is to make it abundantly clear that salvation is "not because of works but because of him who calls."

In our sinful presumption, we have an arrogant assurance that whatever God demands of us, we could do if we really set our mind to do it. We just do not want to do it yet. But when we are ready, we will do what God asks. Election throws a humbling wrench into our arrogance. Election says that our salvation is not in our hands. This is something we do not hear from the preachers who tell us that Jesus is patiently waiting to see whether we will allow him into our hearts. The doctrine of unconditional election reveals a God who is strong and in control—a God who does as he pleases. Election teaches us that we are completely at the mercy of a God whom we have offended.

Some people say, "Okay—even if election is taught in the Bible, we ought not to talk about it, because it will just make sinners throw up their hands and think that there is nothing they can do." That is exactly what election is calculated to do, and that is precisely the attitude that a sinner must have before he can enter the kingdom of heaven. As Luther discovered, despair is so very close to grace.[2]

Read again those verses about Jacob and Esau. God chose Jacob, even though he had done nothing to merit being chosen, and God hated Esau before he was even born. Does that sound just? If it does not sound just, then you have probably understood. The Holy Spirit anticipated that it would seem unjust, for he asks,

> What shall we say then? Is there injustice on God's part? By no means! For he says to Moses, "I will have mercy on whom I have mercy, and I will have compassion on whom I have compassion." (vv. 14–15)

God is not unjust, for he is under no obligation to show mercy or compassion to anyone. To truthfully say that God is unjust to choose Jacob and not Esau, one would have to first prove that God was obligated to choose both. God says, "I will show mercy and compassion to whomsoever I please": "So then it depends not on human will or exertion, but on God, who has mercy" (v. 16).

Again, election strips us of our arrogant presumption—we cannot save ourselves.

> For the Scripture says to Pharaoh, "For this very purpose I have raised you up, that I might show my power in you, and that my name might be proclaimed in all the earth." So then he has mercy on whomever he wills, and he hardens whomever he wills. (vv. 17–18)

---

2. See Martin Luther, *The Bondage of the Will*, trans. J. I. Packer and O. R. Johnston (Grand Rapids: Revell, 1957), 217. See also p. 168.

Here we are confronted with some truths that make our flesh recoil. God raised up Pharaoh to become a mighty ruler for the specific purpose of showing his own power to all the earth when he hardened Pharaoh and subsequently destroyed Pharaoh and his kingdom.

Now that really does seem unjust. God hardened Pharaoh, and then he punished him because of what he did in his hardness? God could have softened him if he had wanted to. Does this seem unjust? Then you have probably understood, for the Holy Spirit anticipates that it would raise such a protest: "You will say to me then, 'Why does he still find fault? For who can resist his will?'" (v. 19).

Many say that God wants every person to be saved, and that he has done and is doing all that he can to make that happen. Do you think he wanted Pharaoh to be saved? Surely Peter was aware of Pharaoh when he wrote that the Lord is "not wishing that any should perish, but that all should reach repentance" (2 Peter 3:9). We must take Pharaoh into account when we interpret that verse. It must mean that God is not willing that any of his elect should perish.

Also, note that the election taught in Romans 9 is drastically different from the version of election that we get in the Tunnel of Time theory. After hearing the Tunnel of Time theory, in which God chooses those who first choose him, no one says, "Hey, wait a second. That is totally unjust!" No— the Tunnel of Time theory perfectly accords with our human ideas of fairness. The Holy Spirit anticipates that when the natural man is confronted with the doctrine of unconditional election, his natural reaction will be a protest of perceived injustice. If your version of election does not sound unjust to the natural man, it is almost certainly not the version of election we have here in Romans 9.

The Holy Spirit does not hurry to soothe our spiritual

sensitivities. He may be a gentleman, but he is an awfully forthright gentleman.

> But who are you, O man, to answer back to God? Will what is molded say to its molder, "Why have you made me like this?" Has the potter no right over the clay, to make out of the same lump one vessel for honorable use and another for dishonorable use? (vv. 20–21)

The Bible may give other answers to why God has elected, but none is more important than the one we have here: God does as he pleases. As I write elsewhere in this chapter, God might use the doctrine of unconditional election to teach us that he does as he pleases, or he might use some other means—but one way or another, we all must learn it.

To the person who has not yet learned to submit to God's sovereignty, the case of Pharaoh is obnoxious. To the person who has learned to submit, the case of Pharaoh is mysterious. Mysterious but gracious—for God's wrath against Pharaoh was only the black background against which he displayed the glistering white diamond of his love for Israel. What if Pharaoh is not the only one God has raised up for the sake of showing his power and glory?

> What if God, desiring to show his wrath and to make known his power, has endured with much patience vessels of wrath prepared for destruction, in order to make known the riches of his glory for vessels of mercy, which he has prepared beforehand for glory—even us whom he has called, not from the Jews only but also from the Gentiles? (vv. 22–24)

What God did to Pharaoh is a picture of what he has been doing throughout the history of the world. He patiently endures the non-elect for the purpose of making his glory and mercy known to those he has called—the elect.

Objections

Loved Ones May Not Be Elect

One of the main reasons that people find the doctrine of unconditional election so offensive is because it entails the very real possibility that a lost loved one may not be one of the elect. Remember, however, that no one seeks God unless God seeks that person first. There is no hope for our lost loved one unless she is elect; that is true—but she may be one of the elect, in which case she will certainly be saved! In hoping and praying for the salvation of your loved one, would you rather put your hope in the possibility that your loved one will come to God on her own (something the Bible declares to be impossible) or in the possibility that God will sovereignly bestow his grace on her?

God Predestined Many People to Hell

Another reason that many people initially recoil from embracing unconditional election is that if election be true, they reason, God has created myriads of people who have no chance of salvation. He created them just so he could destroy them. They protest, "This is not merely unfair; it is monstrous."

If you reject unconditional election and hold to conditional election, it might seem like everyone has a chance to be saved—but to be consistent, you will have to abandon the idea that God knows everything. If God knows everything, then he knows what is going to happen in the future. Is there any possibility that what God knows will happen in the future will somehow not happen the way he foresees it? Of course not. You are then left with a future that cannot be altered, and you end up with the same difficulties that you hoped to avoid by rejecting unconditional election. If God knows that your loved one will not believe, then there is no possibility that she will believe. If God knows that myriads of people will live lives of rebellion against him and consequently be damned forever, and he nevertheless allows them to be born, he is still open to the accusation of being unfair and monstrous.

Related to the foregoing objection is another. If God has predestined some to go to heaven, then he has predestined others to go to hell, and he will send them there merely because they are non-elect. In thinking through this objection, consider two truths.

- Election to everlasting life is *un*conditional, but election to eternal punishment is *conditional*. God has "endured with much patience vessels of wrath prepared for destruction" (Rom. 9:22). He must be patient with them, because they are rebelling against him. According to the Bible, God does not send anyone to hell because that person is non-elect; he sends them to hell because they are sinners who willingly rebel against him.
- Every human deserves God's wrath, and God would be just to send all humans to hell. Is it wrong for God to send rebellious sinners to hell? Then why would it be wrong for him to *plan* to do so?

Belief in Election Kills Evangelism

Yet another objection is that the doctrine of unconditional election kills missions and evangelism. I already addressed this objection in the first chapter (see pp. 20–23), so here I will just give an illustration.

I am a hunter, and I primarily hunt deer and turkeys.

A crucial element of successful hunting entails scouting for evidence that my quarry is actually inhabiting the area I intend to hunt. When hunting for deer, I look for tracks and trails, as well as scrapes and rubs made by bucks. When hunting for turkey, I look for tracks, feathers, and strut zones, and I listen for turkeys. If I find enough signs, I know that that location is a good hunting spot.

But even when hunting in a good spot, most days I do not harvest an animal. Hunting requires a great deal of patience. Some days I do not even see or hear anything, but I do not give up on that hunting location. I will continue to sit or walk quietly for hours hunting my quarry. Why do I keep hunting that area even when I am not successful—and sometimes do not even see anything? Because I know that there are turkeys there. I have confidence that if I keep hunting, sooner or later I will have the opportunity to harvest a turkey.

The doctrine of unconditional election assures us that God has given Christ a people, who are scattered throughout the world. He has given the Good Shepherd a flock of sheep. The entire flock has not yet been brought into the fold, but Jesus said, "All that the Father gives me will come to me" (John 6:37). During his ministry on earth, Jesus predicted the inclusion of yet unconverted Gentile sheep with the sheep of Israel when he said, "I have other sheep that are not of this fold. I must bring them also, and they will listen to my voice. So there will be one flock, one shepherd" (John 10:16). Later he emphasized that "my sheep hear my voice, and I know them, and they follow me" (John 10:27).

When I am hunting turkeys, I use turkey calls. I do not use a deer call or a duck call. I am after turkeys, so I use a turkey call. Similarly, when we are seeking Christ's sheep, let us use the sheep call: the truth of Christ. "My sheep hear my voice." This frees me from the temptation to use psychological manipulation in order to get people to receive Christ. "We have renounced disgraceful, underhanded ways. We refuse to practice cunning or to tamper with God's word, but by the open statement of the truth we would commend ourselves to everyone's conscience in the sight of God" (2 Cor. 4:2). Share the gospel, and the sheep will come.

This also frees me from despair when I do not see the results I might wish. Preaching is my work. Evangelizing is my work. Praying is my work. Salvation is God's work. The one who planned in eternity past to redeem a people for himself will see the job finished. "He who began a good work in you will bring it to completion at the day of Jesus Christ" (Phil. 1:6). This comforts me as a gospel preacher, and it comforts me as a gospel believer. My salvation is the work of the sovereign Lord, who has been planning to save me from before the creation of the world.

Election Seems Inconsistent with the Gospel Call

Finally, it seems that the doctrine of unconditional election is inconsistent with the gospel's promises that "whosoever will may come" and "whoever believes in him should not perish but have eternal life" (John 3:16). Unconditional election, however, does not contradict these gracious promises. It is true that whosoever will may come, but it is also true that no one will come unless the Father who sent Christ draws him to Christ (see John 6:44). Why is anyone willing? "It is God who works in you, both to will and to work for his good pleasure" (Phil. 2:13). Why does anyone put his faith in Jesus? "By grace you have been saved through faith. And this is not your own doing; it is the gift of God" (Eph. 2:8).

There are mysteries that remain in whatever system you believe. I do not want to give the impression that if you embrace the Five Points of Calvinism you will then have all your uncomfortable questions satisfactorily answered. But if we are going to encounter perplexing mysteries in any system, let us encounter them through embracing what is plainly taught in the Scriptures and not because we are trying to explain away what is plainly taught there. God does not need us to defend him.

One of the main benefits of believing in unconditional election is that we are humbled and made to see that salvation must be all of grace, because there is nothing in us that deserves God's favor. There are other ways that God teaches this lesson, but make no mistake about it—everyone who enters the kingdom of God must learn humbly to submit to God's Word and God's will. If we do not learn the lesson of humble submission from the doctrines of God's sovereign grace, we must learn it some other way—but we must learn it.

I do not believe that someone must believe in unconditional election in order to be a Christian. But if someone sees that the Bible teaches unconditional election and refuses to believe what the Lord has plainly revealed, how is it possible that that person has received Christ as his prophet? As a prophet, Christ teaches us the will of God, and his teaching comes to us in the Bible. If we refuse the teaching of the Bible, we are refusing the teaching of the Lord.

A Word about Methodology

Before I became a full-time college professor, I was blessed to be the pastor of three wonderful churches. All three were Bible-believing, pastor-loving churches, and two of those churches believed the Five Points of Calvinism before I became their pastor. In fact, both of these churches wanted a Calvinist pastor, and they probably would not have called someone to be their pastor who was not a Calvinist. In those churches, I enjoyed the privilege of speaking freely and openly about the Five Points. At one of them, I preached a series of sermons on the Five Points. I am sometimes asked to speak at conferences or youth camps that are specifically dedicated to exploring the Five Points, and in those settings I speak frankly and forthrightly about unconditional election. There is a place for that sort of "gloves off," unvarnished, straight-on preaching and teaching on the Five Points.

There are, however, other churches and other settings in which the people who are listening to us speak are hearing these doctrines for the very first time, and they are shocked. Their entire lives they have heard that God wants everyone to be saved. When they hear us saying that God never intended to merely make salvation possible for everyone but planned to make salvation certain for his elect, their theology is shaken to the core.

I am not saying that we ought to keep quiet about what the Bible plainly teaches. False theology leads to false thinking and false faith, and wrong theology needs to be corrected by the truth. I am saying that there are churches and settings in which a more delicate handling of the doctrines of grace is prudent. It is easy for us to be overzealous. When we first see these doctrines in the Bible and embrace them, they are transformative. It is almost like being born again—again! Naturally, we are excited to share with others the truth that has been such a blessing to us. Be wise. Not everything that needs to be said needs to be said right now. With the knowledge of these doctrines comes the responsibility to be a wise soul physician. Most medicine is to be administered gradually and over time. These doctrines are offensive enough to the natural man without making them more offensive through pushy, belligerent arguments. The medicine is already bitter; it is even harder to swallow if it is boiling hot.[3]

Discretion is not deception, nor is it cowardice. Jesus recognized that his disciples were not yet ready to receive everything that they needed to know. "I still have many things to say to you, but you cannot bear them now" (John 16:12). So he waited for the Holy Spirit to reveal these things to them later. If the Lord Jesus could patiently wait for the Holy Spirit to reveal truth, surely you and I can as well.

Someone once asked John Newton,

"Pray, Mr. Newton, are you a Calvinist?" He replied, "Why, sir, I am not fond of calling myself by any particular name in religion. But why do you ask me the question?" "Because, he replied, "sometimes when I read you, and sometimes when I hear you, I think you are a Calvinist; and then, again I think you are not." "Why, sir," said Mr. Newton, "I am more of a Calvinist than anything else; but I use my Calvinism in my writings and my preaching as I use this sugar"—taking a lump, and putting it into his tea-cup, and stirring it, adding, "I do not give it alone, and whole; but mixed, and diluted."[4]

I grew up hearing these doctrines because my father was a faithful, expository preacher of God's Word. During his

3. This statement is adapted from one of the very wisest of soul physicians: "It is too much, says an old writer, to expect that a sick patient will take physic, not only when it is nauseous, but boiling hot" (William Jay, *Morning Exercises for Every Day in the Year* [repr., Harrisonburg, VA: Sprinkle Publications, 1998], 302).

4. George Redford and John Angell James, eds., *The Autobiography of William Jay: With Reminiscences of Some Distinguished Contemporaries, Selections from His Correspondence, Etc.* (1855; repr., Harrisonburg, VA: Sprinkle Publications, 2010), 276.

final days on earth, I read him three of the chapters from this book, and he expressed his hearty approval. He went home to be with the Lord shortly after I commenced working on this chapter.[5] I once asked him, "Dad, did you grow up believing in election?"

"Oh, no," he answered. "I never heard of it until I went to Lexington Baptist College."[6]

"And what did you think of it when you first heard it?"

"It made me so mad I wanted to beat up the boy who talked to me about it."

"How then did you come to believe in election?"

He answered, "Well, it seemed like after that boy talked to me about it, I saw it everywhere in the Bible."

This book may play the part of that boy in your life, dear reader. You, in turn, may be that boy to someone else. But ultimately, the doctrines of grace will be confirmed in the hearts of God's people when they, like my dad, "see it everywhere in the Bible." Therefore, I maintain that the most effective way of teaching these doctrines in the average church is through the faithful, patient exposition of God's Word.[7] If you teach and preach systematically through books of the Bible, you will again and again have opportunity to explain the doctrines of grace, because they are everywhere. In fact, the doctrines of grace are not like fish swimming in a stream of revelation;

5. I did not write the chapters in the order in which they appear in this book.

6. I taught at Lexington Baptist College in the early 1990s, more than thirty years after my dad graduated from there. When Boyce College was formed in 1998, it was blessed to receive many students from LBC, which was just closing. I have taught at Boyce since 2002.

7. For an extended explanation of how to preach and teach expository messages, see Jim Scott Orrick, Brian Payne, and Ryan Fullerton, *Encountering God Through Expository Preaching: Connecting God's People to God's Presence Through God's Word* (Nashville: B&H Academic, 2017).

instead, every doctrine of the Bible is like a fish swimming in a stream of sovereign grace.

Questions for Contemplation and Discussion

1. Why is the doctrine of unconditional election so offensive to the natural man? Why is it offensive to so many genuine Christians?
2. Someone calmly asks, "Why should I believe in the doctrine of election?" Can you give that person three good answers?
3. How has your belief in unconditional election influenced your spiritual life?
4. What does unconditional election reveal about God? About salvation?
5. How does unconditional election affect missions and evangelism?
6. Not only did God choose whom he would save, but he also predestined all the means of their salvation. What are some of those means?
7. Perhaps the most common initial reaction from someone hearing the doctrine of unconditional election is to claim that it is unfair. Explain why it is not unfair.
8. In one sentence, can you summarize the doctrine of unconditional election?

LIMITED ATONEMENT

The Son Secured the Salvation of His People

"A Ransom for Many" (Mark 10:45)

"At what point in *Pilgrim's Progress* does Christian get saved?"

When I ask this question to my students who have just finished reading the book, they nearly always respond with a variety of answers. After batting around several ideas, we narrow the possibilities down to two: Christian was saved either when he entered through the Wicket Gate or when his burden rolled off his back at the cross.

Most students conclude that Christian got saved at the cross, but this is, in fact, the wrong answer. Christian got saved when he entered through the Wicket Gate. Students get the answer wrong because they misunderstand three critical elements of Bunyan's allegory: they misunderstand the Wicket Gate, they misunderstand Christian's burden, and they misunderstand the proper object of saving faith.

The Wicket Gate

A wicket gate is a small or narrow gate, and in the Bible Jesus identifies himself as the narrow gate; so in *Pilgrim's Progress* the Wicket Gate represents Christ. When Christian asks Evangelist, "Whither must I fly?" Evangelist directs Christian to the Wicket Gate, or to Christ, and not to the cross. The Wicket Gate represents Christ.

Christian's Burden

My students usually misunderstand what the burden on Christian's back represents. When we meet him, Christian has an enormous burden on his back, and Christian's burden represents not sin *per se* but the shame and doubt that he feels because of his sin. Christian's sins are forgiven, and he is justified, when he receives Christ—which is represented by his entering the Wicket Gate. But Christian does not yet understand the basis of his forgiveness, so his conscience continues to bother or burden him. Put in more technical terms (which is always a welcome means of clarification), the burden represents *psychological* guilt, not *forensic* guilt. Therefore, what Christian loses at the cross is his shame and doubt caused by sin, because his sins had already been forgiven when he entered the Wicket Gate.

Also, at the cross, Christian receives a scroll, which he later calls his assurance. When Christian enters the Wicket Gate, he receives Christ. When he gazes at the cross, he understands substitutionary atonement and imputed righteousness, and this gives him assurance that his sins are forgiven. This understanding of Christian's salvation in *Pilgrim's Progress* parallels Bunyan's own experience as he describes it in his spiritual autobiography, *Grace Abounding to the Chief of Sinners*. There he informs us that for many months after his conversion he was tormented by deeply unsettling questions about his salvation, but all these questions were put to rest when he came to understand imputed righteousness. So Christian was saved the moment he entered the Wicket Gate, and that was before he came to the cross.

The Proper Object of Saving Faith

This paves the way for us to think about the third error that my students sometimes make: they are confused about the proper object of saving faith. "Are you saying that some-one can be saved without the cross?" a concerned student asks. "No," I answer. "No one can be saved apart from what Jesus accomplished on the cross; but the Bible proclaims that a person gets saved when he receives Christ, and it does not say that a person gets saved through believing that Jesus died for him. Christ himself is the proper object of saving faith, not some part of his work." This is a reflective moment for most, because in these days, it is not uncommon for a person to have been told that if he will believe that Jesus died for him, he will be saved—but I repeat: this is not found in the Bible. A person is saved not when he believes in right doctrine (substitutionary, penal atonement, in this case) but when he believes in the right person—namely, Christ. So the object of saving faith is not a doctrine but a Savior.

I joyfully grant that in receiving the Savior, a person must believe the gospel of the Savior, and the gospel includes the fact that Christ died for our sins in accordance with the Scriptures (see 1 Cor. 15:3), but the gospel includes more than Christ's death! It also includes, for example, the truth that he was "the offspring of David, as preached in my gospel" (2 Tim. 2:8; see also Rom. 1:3). It includes the truths that "he was buried, that he was raised on the third day in accordance with the Scriptures, and that he appeared to Cephas, then to the twelve [and to many others]" (1 Cor. 15:4–5; see also vv. 6–8). There are several essential parts to the gospel message, and a person must believe the gospel in order to be saved, but a part—even an essential part—is not the whole.

It is not biblical to isolate only one element of the gospel and say that if you believe that one element, you have received Christ. Would anyone choose the essential, extracted element of the gospel to be that Christ was a descendent of David? Certainly that is part of the gospel, but no one would say that if a person believes that Christ was a descendent of David he will be saved. What if the isolated element is the resurrection? In Romans 10:9, the Holy Spirit says, "If you confess with your mouth that Jesus is Lord and believe in your heart that God raised him from the dead, you will be saved." This Scripture actually confirms the point I am making. If you confess that Jesus is Lord, it is essential that the Lord is alive. It is impossible to receive a person if he is dead. If Jesus is not raised from the dead, then all we have is a dead doctrinal system. If we are to be saved to the uttermost, we must have a living Savior to continue to do the work of a high priest for us:

> The former priests were many in number, because they were prevented by death from continuing in office, but he holds his priesthood permanently, because he continues forever. Consequently, he is able to save to the uttermost those who draw near to God through him, since he always lives to make intercession for them. (Heb. 7:23–25)

When we believe in Jesus, we affirm what the Bible teaches about who he is and what he did to reconcile us to God, but Christ himself is the treasure chest of salvation. Receive him, and you receive all that is in him. The doctrine of substitutionary, penal atonement is an indispensable, essential component of the gospel, but it is not the whole gospel. How many Christians understood this crucial doctrine when they first received Christ? Nearly none! Yet they were genuinely converted. How? Because, in spite of having underdeveloped or even mistaken ideas about the nature of the atonement, all who receive Christ the risen Lord as Lord and Savior are saved.

Why It Matters

The reader may be puzzled at this point and say, "I thought this was going to be a chapter about the importance of the doctrine of the atonement, but you seem to be asserting that a person may be mistaken about the extent of the atonement and still be a Christian!" That is correct. That is what I am asserting—and, far more significantly, that is what the Bible asserts. Anyone who receives Christ and believes in his name receives the right to become a child of God (see John 1:12). Whoever believes in God's Son will not perish but will have eternal life (see John 3:16). Whoever believes on the Lord Jesus Christ will be saved (see Acts 16:31).

Since this is the case, why all the fuss about the extent of the atonement? I will unfold a number of answers to that question, but none is more significant than the fact that those who hold to false ideas about the extent of the atonement nearly always give a non-biblical answer to the all-important question "What must I do to be saved?" They tell sinners that they must believe that Jesus died for them and that, if they believe this, then they will be saved. This is deadly false. Note the following illustrative passage from one of C. H. Spurgeon's sermons:

> I have sometimes thought when I have heard addresses
> from some revival brethren who had kept on saying time

after time, "Believe, believe, believe," that I should like to have known for myself what it was we were to believe in order to our salvation. There is, I fear, a great deal of vagueness and crudeness about this matter. I have heard it often asserted that if you believe that Jesus Christ died for you you will be saved. My dear hearer, do not be deluded by such an idea. You may believe that Jesus Christ died for you, and may believe what is not true; you may believe that which will bring you no sort of good whatever. That is not saving faith. The man who has saving faith afterwards attains to the conviction that Christ died for him, but is not of the essence of saving faith. Do not get that into your head, or it will ruin you. Do not say, "I believe that Jesus Christ died for me," and because of that feel that you are saved. I pray you to remember that the genuine faith that saves the soul has for its main element—trust—absolute rest of the whole soul—on the Lord Jesus Christ to save me, whether he died in particular or in special to save me or not, and relying, as I am, wholly and alone on him, I am saved. Afterwards I come to perceive that I have a special interest in the Saviour's blood; but if I think I have per- ceived that before I have believed in Christ, then I have inverted the Scriptural order of things, and I have taken as a fruit of my faith that which is only to be obtained by rights, by the man who absolutely trusts in Christ, and Christ alone, to save.[1]

I want to acknowledge with joyful gratitude that many thousands have been genuinely converted through the

1. C. H. Spurgeon, "Knowing and Believing" (sermon no. 3331, Metro- politan Tabernacle, London, September 30, 1866), available in *Metropoli- tan Tabernacle Pulpit*, vol. 58 (1912), 583–84.

ministries of preachers who believe in universal atonement and who are often sloppy and even misleading in their gospel presentations.[2] How can this be? Of course, God is sovereign, and Jesus confidently declared, "All that the Father gives me will come to me" (John 6:37)—but there is another reason. In spite of having misunderstandings about the nature and extent of the atonement, these preachers often point sinners to Christ alone for salvation. Whoever receives Christ is saved. You can believe all the right doctrines and still be lost if you do not receive Christ.[3] Conversely, you can be wrong about a lot of important doctrines and be saved if you receive and rest upon Christ alone for salvation as he is presented in the gospel.[4]

But while it is gloriously true that anyone who hears Jesus's words and believes God who sent Jesus has eternal life and will not be condemned, because he has crossed over from death to life (see John 5:24), John Bunyan discovered, and his character Christian discovered in *Pilgrim's Progress*, that understanding what Jesus accomplished on the cross is the only sufficient ground for quieting an accusing conscience. Understanding the significance of the cross is the only means of relieving sin-burdened Christians, and understanding what happened on the cross will make you feel like Bunyan's pilgrim when he gave three leaps for joy and went on his way singing. I well remember the cold January night when I lay

2. Paul expresses a similar gratitude that Christ was being preached even if the preaching was being done by preachers with significant deficiencies (see Phil. 1:15–18).

3. I know this from personal experience. Being reared in a Bible-rich home, and having an argumentative turn, I was quite the Christian apologist before I was converted at age fourteen.

4. I also know this from personal experience. I received Christ at fourteen, and I did not understand the nature and extent of the atonement until age nineteen.

awake, a lump of joy in my throat, thinking, *I am saved because of what Jesus has already done!* That changes everything.

The Way Ahead

I will consider two intertwined issues regarding the atonement. The first issue is the extent of the atonement. Did Christ die to take away the sins of every human in the world, or did he die to take away the sins of his people only? The second issue is inseparable from the first, and it has to do with the effectiveness of the atonement. Did Christ die to make the salvation of every human possible, or did he die to make the salvation of his elect certain?

I assert that the Holy Spirit teaches in the Bible that Christ died only for the elect and that his death makes the salvation of the elect certain. This doctrine is usually called *limited atonement* in contrast to *universal atonement*, because the benefits of Christ's atoning work are limited to the elect and are not applied to every human. I prefer to call the doctrine *particular redemption* for the same reason that I prefer the term *pro-life* over the term *anti-abortion*. *Particular redemption* better reflects the idea that we are primarily asserting a positive doctrine by emphasizing what Christ accomplished rather than contradicting a false doctrine by emphasizing what he did not.

Before plunging into the argument, let us bear in mind that in discussing this theological issue, we are also thinking about the bloody, painful death of someone we love. I am uneasy with the flippant attitude we sometimes evidence when we sing or preach or write about the sacrifice of Jesus. We simply could never maintain such a casual, detached, irreverent attitude about the death of someone in our family—especially if that loved one gave up his or her life so that we might live. It is, if nothing else, in poor taste to sing a text about the blood of Jesus with a frivolous melody that encourages flippancy and makes reverence unlikely. We ought to be joyful about the cross—but, in the words of Psalm 2, we must "rejoice with trembling" (v. 11). Similarly, it is in poor taste to discuss theological issues surrounding the atonement as if we are simply trying to win a debate.

The Atonement Was Not Offered for Angels

Although most do not realize it, almost everyone who believes the Bible believes that the atoning work of Christ is limited in some way. For example, the Holy Spirit says in Hebrews 2:16 that Christ's work was not offered on behalf of angels: "For surely it is not angels that he helps." Interestingly, I have never known anyone to be distressed about the fact that, as far as we know, God has made no provision for the salvation of these fallen angelic beings and that he will consequently punish them forever because of their sin. To me, it seems inconsistent that someone might protest that God would be unfair if he never provided atonement for every human while the protester never feels any concern about what would seemingly be the even greater unfairness of not providing atonement for even one of the fallen angels.[5]

Not only that, but virtually all Bible believers recognize

---

5. Here is a good question to help clarify the necessity of atonement as the basis for the forgiveness of sin: Suppose the devil were to repent of his sins and his rebellion against God and were to go to God and ask for God's forgiveness. Based on what we read in the Bible, would God forgive him? The answer is no. Why? Because there has been no atonement made for the sin of the devil or of his angels. Without the shedding of blood there is no remission of sin. I heard this illustration from Dr. Jimmy Millikin, longtime professor at Mid-America Baptist Theological Seminary.

that the benefits of the atonement are applied only to those who repent and believe and that, even if he has not chosen them to believe, God knows exactly who will believe, so the end result is that only a certain number of people will be saved by the atonement.[6] All Bible believers hold to some form of limited atonement. It may be limited in its sufficiency, limited in its efficiency, or limited in its application, but it is limited in some way.

I admit, however, that most Christians today do not understand limited atonement in the way I will explain it in this chapter. Even some Five-Point Calvinists for whom I have the utmost respect teach something about the extent of the atonement with which I disagree. They teach that the atonement was sufficient for all, but efficient for the elect. I maintain that the Scriptures teach that the sufficiency and the efficiency of the atonement are coequal, and I will explain why. I hope to convince you of it from the teaching of the Bible. Weigh what I say and see if it is what the Bible teaches. If you conclude that I have misinterpreted the Scriptures, then reject what I say and continue to believe what you think the Bible teaches. If you love God and point sinners to seek salvation by faith alone in Christ alone, then you and I will be friends.

I am a bow hunter, and I have written this chapter during bow season. Perhaps this accounts for the plan that I have adopted for exploring the doctrine of particular redemption. I will first establish the plot of woods where I will hunt. Second, I will identify the particular tree where I will put my stand.

6. As mentioned in the previous chapter, many have never considered that once you grant that God is omniscient—that is, that he knows everything that is going to happen—then what he knows will happen is unfailingly going to happen, and there is no possibility that it will not happen since he knows it is going to happen. Whether he planned the future events or not, the outcome is the same unalterable outcome either way.

Third, I will remove some bushes that might interfere with the flight of my arrows. Fourth, I will shoot three arrows at my target. And, finally, I will prepare the harvest for practical use.

The Plot of Woods

Here is the plot of woods where I will hunt. There are several theories that speculate about the meaning of Christ's death on the cross. I am not going to explore those other plots of woods. Instead, I maintain that the Bible teaches that Christ's death on the cross was a *substitutionary, penal atonement*, and everything that follows in this chapter is based on this understanding of Christ's death.

- It was *substitutionary*—that is, Jesus was taking someone's or some group's place. That is what a substitute does. When you had a substitute teacher in school, the regular teacher was not there, but someone else was there attempting to do the teacher's job.
- It was *penal*—that is, Christ was suffering a penalty, and that penalty was the punishment due to the sins committed by those for whom he was standing as substitute.
- It provided *atonement*. Christ did what the Father required of him, and God was satisfied with him and the sacrifice that he offered. God was reconciled to sinners because of Christ's sacrifice.

Note how the Holy Spirit emphasizes the first two truths—*substitutionary* and *penal*—in Isaiah:

Surely he has borne our griefs
    and carried our sorrows;
yet we esteemed him stricken,

smitten by God, and afflicted.
But he was pierced for our transgressions;
  he was crushed for our iniquities;
upon him was the chastisement that brought us peace,
  and with his wounds we are healed.
All we like sheep have gone astray;
  we have turned—every one—to his own way;
and the Lord has laid on him
  the iniquity of us all. (53:4–6)

The third understanding is described in 2 Corinthians:

All this is from God, who through Christ reconciled us to himself and gave us the ministry of reconciliation; that is, in Christ God was reconciling the world to himself, not counting their trespasses against them, and entrusting to us the message of reconciliation. . . . For our sake he made him to be sin who knew no sin, so that in him we might become the righteousness of God. (2 Cor. 5:18–19, 21)

I stated that all that follows in this chapter is based on this understanding of the nature of Christ's work, but it is also true that everything I have to say follows logically from the understanding that Christ's death was a substitutionary, penal atonement. In other words, the nature of the atonement determines the extent and power of the atonement. This is the plot of woods where I will hunt: Christ's death was a substitutionary, penal atonement.

The Tree

When I bow hunt, I usually hunt from a tree stand. Not every tree in the woods is suitable for a tree stand, however.

In this plot of woods, there are three trees where I may potentially hang my stand. Once we grant that Christ's death on the cross was a substitutionary, penal atonement, we have only three options:

- Christ died to take away all sins of all persons.
- Christ died to take away some sins of all persons.
- Christ died to take away all sins of some persons.

The third is the best tree, but let us examine the first two trees and see why we reject them.

First Tree: All Sins of All Persons

This tree represents the position that most Christians think they hold: that Christ died to take away all sins of all persons. But if Christ died to take away all sins of all persons, then on what basis does God send anyone to hell? Someone answers, "Well, Christ paid the debt, but each sinner has to accept it. If the sinner does not accept the gift, then he has to suffer the penalty for his unbelief." To this I ask, "Is unbelief a sin?" Indeed it is, for "this is his commandment, that we believe in the name of his Son Jesus Christ" (1 John 3:23). Disobedience to God's commandment to believe in Christ is certainly a sin. Did Jesus die for this sin of unbelief? If he did, then why will God punish anyone for it? If Christ stood as a substitute for every human who has ever lived, and if God penalized the sin of every human in Christ, and if Christ's suffering and death brought about atonement, then every human who has ever lived will forever enjoy the reconciliation with God that follows from Christ's work. If, however, some humans go to hell as the Bible describes, then Christ's substitutionary, penal atonement must have been offered on behalf of a group less inclusive than "every human who has ever lived."

We reject this first tree because it would involve God in the injustice of punishing sins twice: once when he punished Jesus for the sins of the unbeliever and again when he punishes the unbelieving sinner for his sins in hell.

Second Tree: Some Sins of All Persons

I have heard it said that Jesus died for every sin of every person except for the sin of persistent unbelief. The person who says this falls into the second category above—that Christ died to take away some sins of all persons. I almost feel like I am attacking a straw man when I argue against this position, but it is the inevitable position of those who hold to an alleged universal atonement while denying universal salvation. As for the theory that Christ died for all sins except persistent unbelief, it is negated by the fact that the Holy Spirit tells us in the Bible that persons are sent to hell for sins other than the sin of unbelief. "Neither the sexually immoral, nor idolaters, nor adulterers, nor men who practice homosexuality, nor thieves, nor the greedy, nor drunkards, nor revilers, nor swindlers will inherit the kingdom of God" (1 Cor. 6:9–10; see a similar list in Gal. 5:19–21).

Furthermore, if Christ died for only some sins, then on what basis are those sins forgiven for which Christ did not die? And, like the first theory, this theory also means that God will have unjustly punished sins twice if he sends sinners to hell because of the sins for which Jesus already suffered the penalty.

So we reject the first two trees, and I will hang my stand from the third: that Christ died to take away all sins of some persons.

Three Interfering Bushes

When a hunter is preparing a hunting site, he must clear some shooting lanes because the smallest branch or vine can divert an otherwise well-shot arrow. There are three commonly held ideas that have the potential to keep a person from hearing what the Holy Spirit says about the extent of the atonement. So before I shoot the arrows that are the basis of my argument, I will attempt to get these three distracting ideas out of the way.

First Bush: "That's Not Fair!"

This bush represents the protest that "it is unfair for Jesus to die for some and not for others."[7] Let me address this concern by asking a question: what does the word *fair* mean? The answer is that it means to give every person his due—to give a person what he deserves or has earned. Now think about this: what does every sinner deserve? What is his due? What has he earned? The Holy Spirit answers that "the wages of sin is death" (Rom. 6:23). Everyone deserves the wrath of God, and no one deserves to have a Savior die for him. Would it be fair for God to send every sinner to hell? Yes! Then why does it become unfair when he graciously rescues some sinners from hell and leaves others to receive the penalty due to their sins?

The Master of the house asks, "Am I not allowed to do what I choose with what belongs to me? Or do you begrudge my generosity?" (Matt. 20:15). Before someone can insist that it is unfair for Jesus to die for some and not for others, he must first prove that every sinner deserves to have Jesus die for him. The Holy Spirit, however, says the exact opposite. No

---

7. Since this protest is so common, I address it more than once in this book. Also, I know that some may read only one chapter.

sinner deserves to have Jesus die for him; rather, every sinner deserves to die for his own sins, and Jesus has no obligation to die for anyone.

Second Bush: "World" and "All"

Another bush that might interfere with my arrows' flight is the assumption that John 3:16 and other Scriptures teach that Jesus died to take away the sins of every human who has ever lived. Along with John 3:16, there are a number of other Scriptures that say that Christ's work was done on behalf of the *world* or for *all*. Here are the most outstanding examples:

For God so loved the world . . . (John 3:16)

He is the propitiation for our sins, and not for ours only but also for the sins of the whole world. (1 John 2:2)

This is good, and it is pleasing in the sight of God our Savior, who desires all people to be saved and to come to the knowledge of the truth. For there is one God, and there is one mediator between God and men, the man Christ Jesus, who gave himself as a ransom for all. (1 Tim. 2:3–6)

And I, when I am lifted up from the earth, will draw all people to myself. (John 12:32)

Therefore, as one trespass led to condemnation for all men, so one act of righteousness leads to justification and life for all men. (Rom. 5:18)

It is alleged that the meaning of the words *world* and *all* in these passages mean *every human who has ever lived*, and that therefore these Scriptures must teach that the atonement was made for every human being who has ever lived. I maintain, however, that the words *world* and *all* in these passages refer to all the people groups of the world, not to every person who has ever lived. That is, the words *world* and *all* mean *all people groups without distinction*; the words do not mean *all persons without exception*.

Sound suspicious? It sounds like I am trying to make Scripture fit my theological system rather than letting Scripture shape my theological system, right? Let us take a closer look. I'll start with an analogy.

Please; not those people. In the area where I grew up, there was a family—I'll call them the Smiths—that included several boys who might be described as rough. The Smith boys wanted everyone to know that they were good fighters, and they were always getting into fights. If we had a neighborhood football game or softball game, and if the Smiths were there, you could bank on it: there was going to be a fight. They smoked everything they could get to burn in a cigarette paper, and they drank everything they could get their hands on—and that was before they got to the seventh grade. It got worse after that. They were notorious thieves and thugs. They were always getting into trouble with the law. My parents told me, "Keep away from them." Their warning was not necessary; I liked my teeth.

But imagine my utter shock if my dad had said to me one day, "Son, you might have heard that Mr. Smith has been sent to the penitentiary. Mrs. Smith cannot take care of all those boys, so your mother and I have decided to adopt them into our family. The Smith boys are about to become your brothers."

After I had established that Dad was not trying to pull some sadistic joke, I would have been dismayed beyond words at the prospect of sharing a house with the Smith boys. Sharing the same neighborhood was dangerous enough. I would have pleaded, "Dad, you have always taught me to make good friends and to keep away from people who will get me into trouble. You know that those Smith boys are nothing but trouble. They will tear up the house, they will steal everything that is not nailed to the floor, they do not eat the food we eat, they do not share our standards of cleanliness, and Dad, if they don't kill me, they will make my life miserable. Please do not do go through with this!"

"Son," my father would respond, "you know that your mother and I love you, but we also love the Smith family. We have determined that we just might be able to do those boys some good, and we are going to try. I understand why you feel the way that you do, but son, it's a done deal. We have already signed the paperwork. The Smith boys are now part of the Orrick family, so move your bed over to that far wall; you will be sharing a room with your new brothers."

Something very similar to that happened in the first century when the Gentiles were adopted into God's family, which up until that point had been almost exclusively a Jewish family. The Jews hated Gentiles, and it was not without reason. The Gentile nations had been brutal to the Jews. Furthermore, for the previous two thousand years, God had been telling the family of Abraham, "Watch out for the Gentiles. Do not marry their daughters. Do not let your daughters marry their sons. When you go into their land, do not merely drive them out; kill them all. Their customs are bad, and their gods are demons. Keep away from the Gentiles."

And then, with the coming of Christ, that policy toward the Gentiles began to change. Before the coming of Christ and his kingdom, you can almost count on one hand the number of Gentiles who are clearly identified in the Bible as being true believers in the living God. Here there is a Rahab, there a Ruth; but the number of Gentile believers under the old covenant is solemnly small.

The first tremors of change were felt during Christ's ministry, but the real earthquake came in the months following the outpouring of the Holy Spirit. Ancient strongholds were cast down; age-old walls of separation were reduced to smoking rubble. God's mercy rushed out upon the world, and the Gentile nations poured into the kingdom of heaven by the thousands. Christ had bound the strong man, and now he began removing from the strong man's house the treasure that rightfully belongs to Christ. It thrills us to think about it—we were the outsiders who are now in the family. The Jews were not so thrilled. I understand. The Smith boys moved in.

If the Smith boys really had moved into my house, my parents would have had to do a whole lot of counseling and explaining and refereeing between parties who had once been enemies and were now brothers living in the same room. It would be naïve to assume that it was all just going to work out. Similarly, the Holy Spirit would have inspired a woefully naïve Christian manual of instruction if he had not included the counseling, explaining, and refereeing necessary for Jews and Gentiles to get along in this kingdom where ethnic distinctives are no longer significant. Not surprisingly, virtually every page of the New Testament is influenced or informed by this very issue. Much of the message of the New Testament will be obscure to the reader who fails to appreciate the enormity and omnipresence of this issue in its pages.[8] It is one

8. I find it significant that the three books of the New Testament that explain the doctrine of justification by faith most clearly—Romans, Galatians, and Ephesians—are also the books in which the Holy Spirit deals most thoroughly with the Jew/Gentile issue. The conflict between Jews and Gentiles provided the perfect backdrop for the gospel of peace to

of the two radically offensive doctrines of the new covenant. (The resurrection of the dead is the other.)

World. This is the mystery hidden for long ages past: the gospel is not just for Jews; it is for all nations, or *the world*, too (see Rom. 16:25–27). The Jews sometimes referred to the non-Jews as *the world*, and it was commonly assumed that when the Messiah came, he would condemn *the world*. So it is no wonder that in his conversation with Nicodemus, who was an ultra pro-Jewish man, Jesus would have to correct his ethnic misunderstandings about the kingdom of God. Like most Jews, Nicodemus assumed that being born a Jew was the only ticket one needed to get into the kingdom. Jesus said that it does not matter what family you were born into; you must be born again or you will never even see the kingdom.

Surely, Nicodemus must have assumed, *God loves Israel and hates the world, for when the Messiah comes he will condemn the world.* Jesus contradicted this thought by saying,

> God so loved the world [*not just the nation of Israel*], that he gave his only Son, that whoever [*whatever person from whatever nation*] believes in him should not perish but have eternal life. For God did not send his Son into the world to condemn the world, but in order that the world might be saved through him. (John 3:16–17)

Remember that the holy men who were moved by the Holy Spirit to write the New Testament, with the possible exception of Luke, were all Jews who had lived under the old way of thinking about Gentiles. Some of them, like the apostle Peter, had a really hard time accepting the fact that the

---

shimmer and the gospel of grace to glisten.

unclean Gentiles had now been pronounced clean by God (see Acts 10 and Gal. 2:11–14). Add to this the fact that some of these Jewish writers were writing their books anticipating that the people who would read their writings would primarily be Jewish Christians. There obviously were Gentile believers in the church at Rome (see Rom. 1:13–15), and yet virtually all the rhetorical arguments that Paul addresses in the book of Romans are arguments that would have been raised by Jews and not by Gentiles.

We do the same sort of thing when we write with a particular readership in mind. A few sentences earlier I wrote, "It thrills *us* to think about it—*we* were the outsiders who are now in the family." When I used the words *us* and *we* in that sentence to refer to Gentiles, I revealed that I am a Gentile and that I expect that most of my readers are Gentiles as well. When I teach English composition, I teach my students that good writers know their readers and write with that group of readers in mind.

As you keep this in mind, read again 1 John 2:2 from the perspective of a Jewish Christian writing to predominantly Jewish Christian readers: "He is the propitiation for our sins, and not for ours only but also for the sins of the whole world." The word *world* in this verse means non-Jews as well as Jews. It does not mean *every human who has ever lived*.

In fact, in the New Testament, the word *world* almost never means *every human who has ever lived*. This is easy to demonstrate even to someone who cannot read Greek. Take an English concordance and count the number of times the word *world* appears in the gospel of John. Depending on the translation on which the concordance is based, *world* will appear between seventy and eighty times. Now go through each of those verses in which the word *world* appears, and when you encounter the word *world*, see if you can replace it with the phrase *every human who has ever lived.* You will discover that you can rarely succeed in this attempted substitution; it just will not make sense.

In my opinion, John never used the word *world* to mean *every human who has ever lived,* but any open-minded reader who candidly investigates the meaning of the word *world* will at least have to admit that the word must usually mean something other than *every human who has ever lived.* Therefore, when the Bible says that God loves the world or that Christ is the propitiation for the sins of the world, it does not necessarily mean that God loves every human who has ever lived and that Christ died to take away every sin of every human who has ever lived. It may well mean that God loves Gentiles as well as Jews and that Christ died for Gentiles as well as Jews.

All. What about the word *all?* Perhaps you have heard preachers dogmatically assert, "All means all, and that's all that all means all the time." Well, as a linguist, I have to say that that is not a very clear way of defining such an important word, and that one ought never to use a word to define itself—but leaving all that to one side, let us see whether "all means all, and that's all that all means all the time." Being a little leery of asking the preachers themselves, who often seem unduly agitated, I must assume that their definition of *all* indicates that only a dunderhead (or a linguist) could fail to see that the word *all* means *every human who has ever lived.*

Let's put it to the test. There is one text where it seems that there is no argument about the meaning of the word *all:* Romans 3:23, which says "For all have sinned and fall short of the glory of God." Surely in this passage the word *all* means *every human who has ever lived,* right? Wrong. And I am not even thinking of the fact that Jesus is an exception to the

statement made in this verse. I am thinking of what has come
before this verse and what comes after it.

> For there is no distinction: for all have sinned and fall short
> of the glory of God, and are justified by his grace as a gift,
> through the redemption that is in Christ Jesus. (vv. 22–24)

All is the subject of the sentence, and there are two statements made about the subject: one, all have sinned; and two,
[all] are justified. If the word *all* means *every human who has
ever lived*, then this verse asserts universalism—the doctrine
that every human will be saved and that no one will go to
hell—because this verse says that all *are justified*, which means
that God has declared them righteous. Not even those who
assert universal atonement assert universal justification. The
word *all* must mean something else in this text, but what?

Notice that last phrase of verse 22: "There is no distinction." No distinction between what or between whom? There
is no distinction between Jews and Gentiles, which has been
the main point of the book of Romans up to this text. You do
not have to read all of the first two and a half chapters to see
this; just read 3:1, 9, 29–30. I believe that every human (except
Jesus) is a sinner, and this is plainly taught in Romans 3:10–18;
but in Romans 3:23, the Holy Spirit is not teaching that every
human is a sinner. Instead, in this text the Holy Spirit is asserting that Jews as well as Gentiles have sinned and that there is
only one way that a person from either party can be justified,
which is through the redemption that is in Christ Jesus. So
even in Romans 3:23 the word *all* does not mean *every human
who has ever lived*.

Jesus said, "And I, when I am lifted up from the earth,
will draw all people to myself" (John 12:32). He said this after
Andrew and Philip told him that there were some Greeks who

wanted to see him (see vv. 20–22). Again, from the context, it is obvious that in using the word *all* Jesus means Gentiles as well as Jews.

Similarly, in 1 Timothy 2:3–6, we read,

> This is good, and it is pleasing in the sight of God our Savior, who desires all people to be saved and to come to the knowledge of the truth. For there is one God, and there is one mediator between God and men, the man Christ Jesus, who gave himself as a ransom for all, which is the testimony given at the proper time.

Again, notice that in the first two verses of this chapter, the Holy Spirit directs that prayers be made "for all people, for kings and all who are in high positions . . . ." The persecuted Christians of the first century may have mistakenly thought that they need not pray for the powerful people who were persecuting them, most of whom were Gentiles—but the Holy Spirit reminds them that there is not one Savior for rich people and another Savior for poor people. There is not a Savior for powerful Gentile pagans and another Savior for poor Jewish Christians. No, there is one God and one mediator between God and men: the man Christ Jesus, who gave himself as a ransom for all—Gentiles as well as Jews. Notice further that in the very next verse, Paul identifies himself as a teacher of the Gentiles (see v. 7).

You can perform the same test on the word *all* as the one I prescribed for the word *world*. Go through a concordance and see how many times you can possibly replace the word *all* with the phrase *every human who has ever lived*, and you will come up with the same result: it almost never can be forced to mean that. So it is certainly not manipulating the texts to say that the words *world* and *all* mean *all people groups without distinction* when these words appear in the texts relevant to the extent of the atonement.

Third Bush: "Sin Is Sin"

A third prevalent idea has the potential to interfere with a ready understanding of the doctrine of particular redemption—a bush that could deflect the flight of my arrows. The potentially interfering idea is that all sins are equally bad in the sight of God. If we think imprecisely about the nature of sin and how God punishes sin, then we might carry this imprecise thinking into our ideas about Christ's substitutionary atonement. This mistaken idea is popularly summarized in the phrase *sin is sin*. It is an interfering bush that needs to be clipped out of the way.

I always encounter this idea when I require my students to read Dante's *Inferno*. In the *Inferno*, Dante assigns specific sinners to specific levels of punishment in hell depending on the severity of their sins. More heinous sins are punished more severely. A student will ask, "Where did Dante get the idea that some sins are worse than others? It is humans who distinguish between bad and worse sins. In the sight of God, sin is sin."

In the discussion that usually follows, I ask students to identify from the Bible those Scriptures that teach that all sins are equally heinous in the sight of God. There are two Scriptures that are consistently alleged to teach this: James 2:10 and Matthew 5:21–48.

In the first passage, James writes, "Whoever keeps the whole law but fails in one point has become guilty of all of it." But James does not say that all sins are equal; instead, he is asserting that perfection is required of anyone who hopes to earn his way to heaven through keeping the law. Mess up one time, and you are done.

In Matthew 5:21–48, a section of the Sermon on the Mount, Jesus compares anger with murder, lust with adultery, and so on. In this section of the Sermon on the Mount, Jesus is pointing out that a person is guilty of sin not only when he does a sinful action but also when he harbors sinful thoughts. God judges the heart as well as the actions. Again, the Scripture does not say that all sins are equally heinous.

And then there is an idea that is persistently brought up, which is that even one sin is sufficient grounds for God to condemn a person to hell. And it is true that even one sin separates a person from God, and that even one sin is sufficient grounds for condemnation, but it does not therefore follow that all sins must be the same in God's sight. Nor does it follow that the punishment for sin in hell is the same for all who suffer there.

The Scriptures clearly teach that all sins are not equally bad in God's sight, but that some sins in themselves are worse than others and that some sins are made worse because of aggravating circumstances.[9] The Scriptures also teach that God punishes specific sins with specific punishments. All sin is terribly bad, and God's judgment against even the least of sins will be horrible, but the Bible teaches that worse sins will receive worse punishments. God's judgment against sin is not *one size fits all.*

When God punishes a sinner, he punishes him neither more nor less than that sinner deserves, and he teaches humans to follow the same principle. The idea that the punishment must fit the crime is the guiding principle behind *eye*

9. Question: "Are all transgressions of the law equally heinous?" Answer: "Some sins in themselves, and by reason of several aggravations, are more heinous in the sight of God than others" (the Baptist Catechism, question and answer 88, and the Westminster Shorter Catechism, question and answer 83).

for an eye and tooth for a tooth (see Ex. 21:24). Our sinful human tendency is to be overzealous in our administration of justice, especially when the offense has affected ourselves or someone we love. If someone maliciously pokes out our eye, we want to cut off his head! But God says, "No, no—you may not cut off his head. The limit is *an eye for an eye.* The punishment must fit, and not exceed, the crime." Here are a few of the Scriptures that teach that not all sins are equally bad in God's sight and that God makes the punishment fit the crime.

> Jesus answered [Pilate], "You would have no authority over me at all unless it had been given you from above. Therefore he who delivered me over to you has the *greater sin.*" (John 19:11)

> And he said to me, "Son of man, do you see what they are doing, the great abominations that the house of Israel are committing here, to drive me far from my sanctuary? But you will see still *greater abominations.*" (Ezek. 8:6; see also vv. 12–13, 15)

Surely there is something unusually bad about blasphemy against the Holy Spirit that sets this sin above other sins:

> Therefore I tell you, every sin and blasphemy will be forgiven people, but the blasphemy against the Spirit will not be forgiven. And whoever speaks a word against the Son of Man will be forgiven, but whoever speaks against the Holy Spirit will not be forgiven, either in this age or in the age to come. (Matt. 12:31–32)

In the following passage, notice how the Lord teaches that worse sins will receive worse punishments:

I tell you, it will be more bearable on that day for Sodom than for that town.

Woe to you, Chorazin! Woe to you, Bethsaida! For if the mighty works done in you had been done in Tyre and Sidon, they would have repented long ago, sitting in sackcloth and ashes. But it will be more bearable in the judgment for Tyre and Sidon than for you. And you, Capernaum, will you be exalted to heaven? You shall be brought down to Hades. (Luke 10:12–15)

Rejection of God's truth is a bad sin, but it is even worse if you reject God's truth when God's Son has done mighty works before your very eyes!

In the following Scripture passage, notice how the disobedient servant is given a more severe punishment because he knew his responsibility and still did not do it:

And that servant who knew his master's will but did not get ready or act according to his will, will receive a severe beating. But the one who did not know, and did what deserved a beating, will receive a light beating. Everyone to whom much was given, of him much will be required, and from him to whom they entrusted much, they will demand the more. (Luke 12:47–48)

Finally, let this next text remind you of all the other places in the Bible where we are informed that God judges *sins* (in the plural) and not just *sin* (in the aggregate): "Alexander the coppersmith did me great harm; the Lord will repay him according to his deeds" (2 Tim. 4:14).

When we understand that God deals out specific punishments for specific sins, we are a step closer to being able to think about what the Scripture says about the extent of the atonement. If God is very exact in his administration of justice against sinners and the sins they commit, then we ought to expect that he would also be exact in his administration of justice against Christ when he stood as a substitute for sinners and bore our sins (plural) in his body on the tree (see 1 Peter 2:24).

Three Arrows

Now that we have thought through some common misconceptions, we are ready to consider three main arguments in support of the truth that when Jesus died on the cross, he died to make the salvation of his elect certain—not to make the salvation of all persons possible. In keeping with my hunting analogy, these three arguments are like three arrows. The first arrow is proof texts, the second arrow is the tone of the New Testament Scriptures, and the third arrow is the word pictures that the Holy Spirit uses to describe the atoning work of Christ.

First Arrow: Proof Texts

The Holy Spirit teaches us in quite a number of Scriptures that Christ's atoning work was offered on behalf of a specific group, and the group identified is less inclusive than every member of the human race. "She will bear a son, and you shall call his name Jesus, for he will save his people from their sins" (Matt. 1:21). The phrase *his people* does not refer to Jesus's own ethnic group, the Jews; instead, *his people* are those from the human race whom the Father has given to him to be his special possession. In John 10 Jesus calls his people *his sheep* when he says, "I am the good shepherd. The good shepherd lays down his life for the sheep" (v. 11). And he makes it clear that he will gather his flock of sheep from both Jewish and non-Jewish nations:

> I am the good shepherd. I know my own and my own know me, just as the Father knows me and I know the Father; and I lay down my life for the sheep. And I have other sheep that are not of this fold. I must bring them also, and they will listen to my voice. So there will be one flock, one shepherd. (vv. 14–16)

In other places, Christ refers to his people as *those whom the Father has given me*. Jesus said, "All that the Father gives me will come to me, and whoever comes to me I will never cast out" (John 6:37). When Jesus acts as a high priest on behalf of his people, part of his responsibility is to pray for them. Notice for whom he prays: "I am praying for them. I am not praying for the world but for those whom you have given me, for they are yours" (John 17:9). If God wants every person to be saved, why would he give Jesus only some persons to be his people, and why would Jesus pray only for his own while specifically pointing out that he was not praying for the others? The answer is that Christ came to save his people from their sins.

In Revelation, Christ's people are called his *bride* (see 19:6–8; 21:9), and in Ephesians we read how he won this bride for himself and made her ready to be his bride:

> Christ loved the church and gave himself up *for her*, that he might sanctify her, having cleansed her by the washing of water with the word, so that he might present the church to himself in splendor, without spot or wrinkle or any such thing, that she might be holy and without blemish. (Eph. 5:25–27)

Here Christ is said to have given himself up for *the church*, and while the church includes persons from the entire world, the church is not every person in the world.

Jesus said, "For even the Son of Man came not to be served but to serve, and to give his life as a ransom *for many*" (Mark 10:45). Christ was "offered once to bear the sins *of many*" (Heb. 9:28).

There are other Scriptures in which the Holy Spirit teaches that Christ's work was offered on behalf of a group less inclusive than every person who has ever lived, but my favorite is Romans 8:32. "He who did not spare his own Son but gave him up for us all, how will he not also with him graciously give us all things?" It may not be readily apparent why I bring up this Scripture as a proof text for particular redemption. In fact, those who disagree with me about the extent of the atonement might point out that this text says that God gave his son for *us all!* But follow the line of the Holy Spirit's reasoning in this verse. He reasons from the greater to the lesser, and his argument may be paraphrased this way: "If God gave such an enormous gift for the salvation of sinners— the sacrifice of his only Son—does it not stand to reason that he will also give all the lesser gifts that are necessary for this greater gift to be effective?"

Let me illustrate. Suppose that I were wealthy enough to give one of my daughters a Rolls-Royce automobile as a birthday gift. On the day that I hand her the keys, she exclaims, "Oh, thank you so much, Dad, but I cannot afford the insurance on this car, and I do not know how I am going to afford the gas, either." I would respond, "Don't worry; I'll take care of it. After all, if I love you enough to spend all this money to give you this nice car, I love you enough to make sure that you can enjoy it. The price of insurance and the cost of gasoline are nothing in comparison to what I have already invested in this car."

This is exactly the Holy Spirit's line of reasoning in Romans 8:32. The great, massive sacrifice of God's own Son has already been offered. The enormous purchase has been made. What is the gift of repentance in comparison to the gift of God's Son? What is the gift of faith in comparison to the gift of God's Son? What is the gift of perseverance in comparison to the gift of God's Son? They are tiny in comparison to the gift of God's Son, and yet these gifts of repentance, faith, and perseverance are necessary for us to enjoy God's Son. We must have repentance and faith. God says, "I'll take care of it. I did not spare my own Son. I will give you all that you need to enjoy him."

Look at the statements surrounding Romans 8:32. "Those whom he predestined he also called, and those whom he called he also justified, and those whom he justified he also glorified" (v. 30). God says, "I'll take care of it." From verse 31 to the end of the chapter, the Lord promises the final perseverance of those for whom Christ died. Again, he is saying, "I'll take care of it."

Verse 32 says that God gave his Son for *us all*. Who is *us all*? Well, one thing is certain: whoever it is will get everything needed to be in heaven forever. It must be so, or the entire argument of the passage collapses. Since every human who has ever lived does not receive the lesser gifts necessary to enjoy the greater gift, we must induce that the greater gift was not offered for the salvation of every human who has ever lived. But those for whom the greater gift was offered will without doubt receive the comparatively lesser gift of *all things*.

Second Arrow: Tone

A new way to see. Throughout my lifetime, I have had an interest in knowing the names of trees, plants, flowers, birds, constellations, and other things that fill the woods and fields and skies where I live. I have noticed something: once I learn the name of a constellation or the name of bird or flower, I see it in a way that I have not seen it before, and I see it more often than I have seen it before. Of course, the thing does not suddenly begin to occur more frequently after I have learned its name, but I have a heightened sense of its presence. I have observed the same pattern with respect to words, doctrines, and ideas: once I learn a new word or gain a fresh perspective on an old idea, it seems to appear everywhere. I propose that the arrow I am about to shoot has the potential to be like that in the minds of those who read the New Testament. Once you see what I am talking about, you will probably see it everywhere in the Bible.

A tone of certain victory. A king of Syria once sent a threatening message to the king of Israel. In the message, the king of Syria adopted a boastful tone, sounding as if he had already won the battle that was yet to be fought. The king of Israel answered, "Tell him, 'Let not him who straps on his armor boast himself as he who takes it off'" (1 Kings 20:11). The king of Israel was a bad man, but he spoke wisely. A person ought not to adopt a tone of certain victory before the battle has even started.

Christ, however, has already won the battle for the souls of his people, and he justly boasts as one who takes his armor off when he proclaims his victory over Satan, sin, and death. Because of the work of Christ, God cancelled "the record of debt that stood against us with its legal demands. This he set aside, nailing it to the cross. He disarmed the rulers and authorities and put them to open shame, by triumphing over them in him" (Col. 2:14–15).

It is no wonder then that when the Holy Spirit speaks in the New Testament about the atoning work of Christ, he speaks about it with a tone of certain, victorious accomplishment and not with a tone of uncertain potential. That is, the Holy Spirit consistently speaks as if the work of Christ actually secures the salvation of sinners. He does not speak about Christ's work as if there were the slightest possibility that his work might be ineffective in saving sinners. But if Christ died for every human who has ever lived, then his death is, in fact, ineffective in the overwhelming majority of cases, for "many are called, but few are chosen" (Matt. 22:14). Christ himself proclaims, "The gate is narrow and the way is hard that leads to life, and those who find it are few" (Matt. 7:14). If Christ died for the purpose of taking away the penalty for the sins of every person who ever lived, he has not accomplished his purpose, and the confident tone of the Holy Spirit is unwarranted.

There are some who believe that Christ died for the sins of every human, but that because of God's sovereign purpose, only the elect are effectually called. If this be true, it is the work of the Holy Spirit and not the work of Christ that distinguishes God's elect from the rest of mankind. While I agree that the Holy Spirit effectually calls the elect alone, I do not believe that this explains the tone of victorious accomplishment that characterizes the New Testament teaching about the effectiveness of Christ's work. Christ's work (not the Holy Spirit's) is consistently presented as the legal basis for the salvation of sinners. This tone of certain victorious accomplishment makes sense only if Christ's work actually secured the salvation of his people. It does not make sense if his work made their salvation merely possible through the subsequent work of the Holy Spirit.

A few examples. This tone of certain victorious accomplishment is so overwhelmingly characteristic of what the Holy

Spirit says about Christ's work that I am hopeful that only a few examples will suffice to show you what I mean. Perhaps then you too will begin to see it everywhere and will realize its implications. "After making purification for sins,[10] he sat down at the right hand of the Majesty on high" (Heb. 1:3). Why did Christ sit down? He has been enthroned in a position of superiority (see v. 4), he is waiting for his enemies to be made his footstool (see v. 13), and he has victoriously finished making purification for sins:

> And every priest stands daily at his service,[11] offering repeatedly the same sacrifices, which can never take away sins. But when Christ had offered for all time a single sacrifice for sins, he sat down at the right hand of God, waiting from that time until his enemies should be made a footstool for his feet. For by a single offering he has perfected for all time those who are being sanctified. (Heb. 10:11–14)

Earlier we saw, in Romans 8:32, that the Holy Spirit argues from the greater to the lesser when he reasons that since God did not spare his own Son we may be sure that he will also give us all things. In the following passage, the Holy Spirit argues the other way around, from the lesser to the greater, to assert the effectiveness of Christ's work on behalf of sinners.

> God shows his love for us in that while we were still sinners, Christ died for us. Since, therefore, we have now been

---

10. Note, again, that the text specifies sins (plural) and not merely sin in general.

11. The fact that every old covenant priest *stands* at his service is contrasted with Christ's sitting. Christ's sitting is cited as evidence that he finished his work of atonement.

justified by his blood, much more shall we be saved by him from the wrath of God. For if while we were enemies we were reconciled to God by the death of his Son, much more, now that we are reconciled, shall we be saved by his life. (Rom. 5:8–10)

In Romans 8:32 we saw that the greater thing was Christ's death. Here in Romans 5 Christ's death is the lesser thing. That sounds almost blasphemous—what could be greater than Christ's death? The passage tells us: *the life* of the risen Christ! Here is a generous paraphrase: "Look—God loved you, and Christ died for you when you hated God. He forgave you and received you into his favor because of his Son's death. But now his Son is alive, and he is representing you before his Father. Do you think God is going to value the sacrifice of his dying Son more than the life of his risen Son? If God forgave you because of his Son's death when you were his enemy and you hated him, how much more, now that you are his child and you love him, will he save you because of his Son's life?"

The whole argument of the passage is founded on the idea that after having died for his people the risen Christ continues to represent them before the Father, and his work, both in death and in life, is effective for their salvation. Again we see that if we apply the argument of this passage to a general atonement, we end up having to assert universal salvation. But if we apply the argument to a particular redemption, we end up with a powerful ground for the assurance of the believer: not only did Christ die for you, he now lives for your benefit.

Turn to virtually any passage of Scripture that speaks of Christ's death, and ask this question: "In this passage, does the Holy Spirit speak of the effects of Christ's death as if there were the least uncertainty about his death being effective, or does he speak of Christ's death with a tone of victorious certainty that his death is effective?" I have no fear of what you will find. This confident tone of certain victorious accomplishment makes sense only if Christ's death effectively secured the salvation of those for whom it was offered. When Jesus cried out, "It is finished!" he meant it.

Third Arrow: Word Pictures

The Holy Spirit has given us quite a few word pictures to help us understand the nature and extent of Christ's atoning work. These word pictures provide some of the most convincing evidence that Christ died to make the salvation of his elect certain.

Christ's work is called a ransom. Jesus said that he "came . . . to give his life as a ransom for many" (Mark 10:45), and the Holy Spirit says that Christ Jesus "gave himself as a ransom for all" (1 Tim. 2:6).

What is a ransom? We usually hear about ransoms in connection with kidnappings. Some bad men kidnap the child of wealthy parents, and then the bad men send a ransom note saying that if the parents pay a ransom price, the child will be released unharmed. When the parents pay the ransom, what ought to happen? The child ought to be released, right? If the bad men do not release the child when the ransom has been fully paid, then in addition to being kidnappers, they are also liars. They said they would release the child when the ransom was paid.

Now let us apply this reasoning to the atonement. Christ's sacrifice was a ransom paid to God the Father, who in his justice had been holding rebellious sinners accountable for their actions. What are the implications if Christ pays their ransom and they do not go free? Did Christ fail to pay the required ransom? Did the Father change his demands and say that something more is required? If Christ paid the ransom for every human who ever lived, why does not God's justice release every sinner? The answer is that Christ did not die as a ransom for every human, but he did die as a ransom for his people, and every one of his people will be saved. The ransom guarantees it.

Christ's death brings about redemption. Redemption means that something has been bought with a price.

So, for example, let us suppose that a young, irresponsible, first-century Roman has accumulated a debt so enormous that he cannot pay it back. In those days, debtors were not sent to prison; they were sold to help pay back the debt. Let us further suppose that a kindhearted benefactor has gone to the slave auction for the purpose of purchasing and adopting a slave. When the young man is put up for auction, the benefactor pays the full price for the slave; he pays the complete price of redemption. What ought to happen next? The young man ought to be released to him. The man bought him. If the man redeemed every slave on sale that day, then every slave ought to be released to him.

The price of our redemption from sin was high: God's own Son had to become a curse for us. Jesus paid it all.

> Christ redeemed us from the curse of the law by becoming a curse for us—for it is written, "Cursed is everyone who is hanged on a tree"—so that in Christ Jesus the blessing of Abraham might come to the Gentiles, so that we might receive the promised Spirit through faith. (Gal. 3:13–14)

> But when the fullness of time had come, God sent forth his Son, born of woman, born under the law, to redeem those

who were under the law, so that we might receive adoption as sons. And because you are sons, God has sent the Spirit of his Son into our hearts, crying, "Abba! Father!" So you are no longer a slave, but a son, and if a son, then an heir through God. (Gal. 4:4–7)

If Jesus paid the redemption price for every human who has ever lived, then every human ought to be released eternally from his slavery, because by his blood Christ our high priest has secured "an eternal redemption" (Heb. 9:12). But Christ did not die to redeem every human. He died to redeem his people, and every one of them will be his. He bought them, paying the full price of redemption.

Christ's sacrifice is a propitiation.

> Christ Jesus, whom God put forward as a propitiation by his blood . . . (Rom. 3:24–25)

> Therefore he had to be made like his brothers in every respect, so that he might become a merciful and faithful high priest in the service of God, to make propitiation for the sins of the people. (Heb. 2:17)

> He is the propitiation for our sins. (1 John 2:2)

What is propitiation? The concept is not unique to Christianity—Greek and Roman mythology are full of instances of propitiation.

Here is the way it works. One of the gods gets upset with a human for some reason. The human does not want the god to be angry anymore, so he offers a sacrifice to appease the god and propitiate or satisfy the god's anger. If the human has offered the sacrifice as the god requires, and if the god is not totally capricious, then the god accepts the propitiatory sacrifice and blesses the human with his favor. That whole system of paganism was a fraud, but they understood propitiation.

In real, true religion, Christ offered himself as a propitiatory sacrifice to God the Father. He offered exactly the sacrifice that God required, and he did it in the way that God prescribed. God is not capricious. He will not maintain his anger against those humans for whom the propitiatory sacrifice was offered.

Other word pictures. I have provided three examples of word pictures that indicate that Christ's sacrifice was effectual for the salvation of sinners. There are many more examples. Briefly consider the following:

- Christ is a Savior: "Our Savior, Christ Jesus" (2 Tim. 1:10). Is a person considered a savior if he merely attempts to save but does not succeed?
- Christ is a Mediator: "There is one mediator between God and men, the man Christ Jesus" (1 Tim. 2:5). Is he a successful mediator?
- Christ is a High Priest: "We have such a high priest" (Heb. 8:1). Is his work accepted?
- Christ is a Good Shepherd: "The good shepherd lays down his life for the sheep" (John 10:11). Does the wolf get some of the sheep anyway?
- Christ is a protecting husband to his bride: "Husbands, love your wives, as Christ loved the church and gave himself up for her" (Eph. 5:25). Does she end up marrying someone else?

A Proper Use of the Doctrine

It is a great blessing to my family and me when I successfully harvest a deer. Much of the meat we eat during the year comes from the deer I kill during deer season. So far this season, I have put several deer in the freezer, and we will eat every bit of the meat. I also brain tan deer hides and use the resulting buckskin to make some of my hunting clothing and other accoutrements. Deer hunting is more than an enjoyable hobby to me; it is practical and beneficial to my family. It puts meat on the table. Getting the deer ready for the table requires some work, however, and this accounts for the proverb "Whoever is slothful will not roast his game" (Prov. 12:27). Part of ethical hunting is putting forth the effort to make a proper use of the game that is harvested.

What is a proper use of the doctrine of particular redemption? Someone might ask, "Even if particular redemption is taught in the Bible, since it is so controversial, wouldn't it be best just to keep quiet about it?" If it is taught in the Bible, it is profitable, and we ought not to keep quiet about it.

> All Scripture is breathed out by God and profitable for teaching, for reproof, for correction, and for training in righteousness, that the man of God may be complete, equipped for every good work. (2 Tim. 3:16–17)

I should hope that I have made it clear that embracing the doctrine of particular redemption has significant ramifications—but allow me to explicitly point out a few.

Assurance of Salvation

The doctrine of particular redemption lays the only solid foundation for the believer to enjoy assurance of his salvation. Consider the alternative: if God the Father loves everyone just the same, if Christ died for everyone who has ever lived, and if the Holy Spirit draws everyone equally, then when you get saved, who has made the difference? You did—and you can boast about it! The downside of this is that if you earned salvation through your merits, you can lose it through your demerits. But if God the Father chose you before the foundation of the world, if Christ died to take away your sins and their penalty, and if the Holy Spirit effectually drew you to Christ, then your salvation rests upon the sovereign work of the omnipotent God, and you are secure forever because of what Christ has already done. How can you know that all these blessings are yours? If you have received Christ, you may be assured that all these blessings are yours. "For all the promises of God find their Yes in him" (2 Cor. 1:20).

A Full Gospel

The doctrine of particular redemption and the other doctrines of God's sovereign grace are part of the biblical gospel, and the gospel is the power of God for the salvation of everyone who believes. So many today are preaching a weak gospel that leaves sinners with the impression that God has done all he can do and that the decisive action is now left up to the sinner. "God really hopes you make the right choice, but he has already done all that he can do. The rest is up to you." This false message leaves the sinner with the idea that he, the sinner, is in control of his salvation and that he will almost be doing God a favor if he takes pity on Jesus and opens the door of his heart. This is not a message that is likely to produce the deep repentance and humility that lead a person to cry out, "God, be merciful to me, a sinner!" However, the truth that God is in control and that he saves whom he pleases helps the sinner to see that he is at the mercy of a holy God who is justly angry against sinners. Then the sinner is ready to receive with humble appreciation the good news that Jesus has provided a certain salvation for all who believe in him. He initiates with us, and we respond to him.

Confidence in Christ

When we understand the doctrine of particular redemption, it is more likely that we will present the true gospel that salvation is through believing in Christ himself and not through believing something about Christ's work. Specifically, we will stop telling people that if they believe that Jesus died for them they will be saved, and we will be more zealous than ever to tell people what the Bible says—that if they believe the whole gospel and receive Christ as Lord and Savior, they will be saved.

Responding to Objections

Earlier, I devoted a section of this chapter to "clipping bushes," and the bushes represented ideas that might interfere with a person's receiving the doctrine of particular redemption. As I close this chapter, I will consider a few objections that might occur to someone who has an open mind to receive the doctrine but who still has some concerns.

Was Jesus's Suffering Limited as Well?

Objection: Particular redemption entails the notion that if one of God's elect had committed one more sin, then Christ's suffering would have been increased to pay for that sin.

I fail to see why this is a ridiculous notion. God does not consider all sins to be equally heinous. When he punishes sin in humans, the punishment fits the crime, and this is true both in time and in eternity. It has been said that a person damned in hell will wish that he had committed one less sin. Christ bore our *sins* in his body, and he made purification for our *sins*. If we were to suffer for our sins, God would punish us neither more nor less than our sins deserved; so when Christ stood as our substitute and bore our penalty, why would we expect God's standards of justice to change?

In saving sinners through Christ, God displays his righteousness because he is so particular in the administration of his justice. Even the "former sins" committed by Old Testament saints were punished in Christ. God's people

> are justified by his grace as a gift, through the redemption that is in Christ Jesus, whom God put forward as a propitiation by his blood, to be received by faith. This was to show God's righteousness, because in his divine forbearance he had passed over former sins. It was to show his righteousness at the present time, so that he might be just and the justifier of the one who has faith in Jesus. (Rom. 3:24–26)

God forgives sinners of their sins because their sins have been paid for. In this way, the accuser of the brethren is cast down, and no one can lay any charge against God's elect. "In Christ God was reconciling the world to himself, not counting their trespasses against them" (2 Cor. 5:19).

God punished Christ for the sins that he was bearing. He did not punish him less than the sins deserved. That would be inconsistent with perfect justice. He did not punish him more than the sins deserved. That too would be inconsistent with perfect justice. What possible benefit would there be to anyone for God to punish Christ more than was necessary to purify his people from their sins? It would not bring glory to God, it would be unnecessarily cruel to Christ, and it would do no good whatsoever for the non-elect.

Is It Even Possible for the Value of Jesus's Suffering to Be Limited?

> *Objection:* How can you limit the value of the suffering of God's own Son—the second person of the Trinity?

Christ had infinite capacity to suffer, but it does not necessarily follow that what he suffered was of infinite value. Can the Infinite One do nothing by measure?[12] Because God has infinite creative power, it does not necessarily follow that he must always be creating. He can create for six days and then stop. A truck capable of hauling two tons can haul one ton. Just because an athlete can bench press four hundred pounds does not mean that he presses that much every time he works out on the bench. How much does he press? As much as his trainer puts on the bar.

Similarly, just because Christ has a divine nature as well as a human nature and is therefore a person who possesses infinite capacity to suffer punishment, it does not mean that he bore more of God's wrath than was necessary to secure our forgiveness and pardon. How much did he bear? As much as God's perfect justice put on the cross.

---

12. "It is a non-sequitur to move from the deity of the sacrifice to sufficiency for every individual man. Such a conclusion assumes that deity can perform nothing by measure" (Thomas J. Nettles, *By His Grace and for His Glory: A Historical, Theological, and Practical Study of the Doctrines of Grace in Baptist Life*, rev. ed. [Cape Coral, FL: Founders Press, 2006], 346).

Why Are the Elect Born Condemned?

Objection: You maintain that Christ's work does not merely make salvation possible but actually saves his elect. You further maintain that it would be unjust for God first to punish a sinner's sin in Christ and then later to punish the sinner himself in hell for the same sin. Don't we have the same problem created by the fact that when the redeemed (but not yet justified) elect are born into this world, they are born sinners under God's condemnation and must be born again in order to enter the kingdom of God? If Jesus secured their salvation, then why are the elect born under God's condemnation and wrath? Jesus said, "Whoever does not believe is condemned already, because he has not believed in the name of the only Son of God" (John 3:18). Paul writes that we "were by nature children of wrath, like the rest of mankind" (Eph. 2:3). Jesus died to pay for the sins of the elect, yet they are born in sin and under condemnation. Isn't this unjust?

There is a significant difference between the real injustice of punishing sins twice and the seeming incongruity of the redeemed elect being born under a temporary sentence of condemnation. The redeemed elect will never have to suffer God's wrath for their sin, but the damned will. While Christ's people are not born saved, their salvation is certain. Though they are born under a sentence of condemnation, their pardon is assured, and their eternal destiny is never in question. This objection is founded on the same principle that may lead us to ask why God would choose his elect before the foundation of the world, destining them for eternal glory, but would nevertheless decree that his elect, along with the entire human race, would fall into sin and thereby bring so much misery into the world he had yet to create. Apparently, God receives more glory through healing a broken world than he would have received had he chosen to reign over an unbreakable one. Similarly, God gets more glory through the regeneration, justification, and sanctification of his redeemed people than he would have received had he arranged for them to be born sinless and already justified.

I really enjoy wearing wool clothing, and I especially enjoy a good pair of wool socks. A pair of socks made of good, quality wool will last a very long time. They do, however, eventually get holes, and the first places my socks develop holes are on the heel and on the toe. I have repaired several pairs of my favorite socks by darning the holes in them. When I darn a pair of socks, I use wool yarn to weave a little patch to cover the hole. I sometimes use a bright red yarn to make the repairs even though the socks may be gray or green. I use bright red yarn because I enjoy seeing the work I have done to repair the damaged socks. In fact, I like my repaired socks more than I like the socks that have never needed to be repaired. When a future child of God is born into this world, he is born a sinner. God gets great glory through repairing each one, and because of the application of Christ's work to us by the Holy Spirit, we are more precious in God's sight than if we had been born perfectly sinless and already justified.

As an illustration of the idea that our redemption has been paid by Christ but that we are still born sinners, suppose that a wealthy grandparent established a million-dollar trust fund for his yet-to-be-born grandson. The trust fund was kept a secret, and the money would not become available to the grandson until his twenty-fifth birthday. Now imagine that the young man lived an irresponsible lifestyle and accumulated so much debt that he was in court on his twenty-fifth birthday and was about to be sentenced to prison. But before the judge's sentence was pronounced, the young man's lawyer came rushing into the courtroom waving some papers and shouting, "His debt has been paid! He has just received a million dollars!" The provision for the payment of his debt had been made before he was born, but it was not his until the appointed time. So it is with the payment that Christ has made for the release of his people. It was made before we were born, but it is not applied to our case until we receive Christ.

The following chart lists four possible ways of understanding the relationship between Christ's death and the justification of those who are eventually saved.

Arminianism	Christ died for every human, but the justification of no one is certain.
Four-Point Calvinism	Christ died for every human, and the future justification of the elect is certain because of God's election and the Holy Spirit's effectual calling.
Hyper-Calvinism	Christ died only for the elect who were, in fact, justified in eternity past.
Biblical Teaching	Christ died only for the elect, thereby ensuring the future justification of the elect through faith.

How Do We Present the Gospel?

Objection: How do we present the gospel to sinners? Since Christ did not die for every human, we cannot know whether or not Christ died for the person(s) we are talking to, so we cannot tell them that Jesus died for them.

Present the gospel the way that it is presented in the Bible. Not once in the Bible do we read of someone saying, "Christ died for you, therefore you ought to receive him." And we saw earlier that Christ himself, and not some part of his work, is the object of saving faith. The Bible does not say that if a person believes that Jesus died for him, he will be saved. If the Bible does not say it, then neither should we. Present the truth about Christ and the work he has done for the salvation of sinners. Freely invite all persons to trust in Christ, and assure them that Jesus will receive anyone who comes to him. Jesus said that he would (John 6:44)! "The Spirit and the Bride say, 'Come.' And let the one who hears say, 'Come.' And let the one who is thirsty come; let the one who desires take the water of life without price" (Revelation 22:17).

This is indeed a doctrine to make a Christian's burden fall off his back. With Bunyan's pilgrim, we too may give three leaps for joy and go on our way singing.

Questions for Contemplation and Discussion

1. What is limited in Limited Atonement?
2. Which is more limited: a universal atonement that guarantees the salvation of no one, or a particular redemption that guarantees the salvation of some? A wide bridge that reaches only halfway to God, or a narrow bridge that reaches all the way to God?[13]

13. "Now, beloved, when you hear any one laughing or jeering at a limited atonement, you may tell him this. General atonement is like a great wide bridge with only half an arch; it does not go across the stream: it only professes to go half way; it does not secure the salvation of anybody. Now, I had rather put my foot upon a bridge as narrow as Hungerford, which went all the way across, than on a bridge that was as wide as the world, if it did not go all the way across the stream" (Charles H. Spurgeon,

3. The Bible teaches that our Lord's death was a substitutionary, penal atonement, and the author asserts that "the nature of the atonement determines the extent of the atonement." Can you explain this statement?

4. The author identifies three ideas that interfere with a ready acceptance of the doctrine of limited atonement. Can you identify others?

5. It is commonly asserted that "if you believe that Jesus died for you, you will be saved." C. H. Spurgeon said, "Do not get that into your head, or it will *ruin* you." Spurgeon's warning is unusually strong. What is so potentially ruinous in this statement?

6. In one sentence, can you summarize the doctrine of Limited Atonement?

"Particular Redemption," in *New Park Street Pulpit* [London, 1859; repr., Pasadena, TX: Pilgrim Publications, 1981], 4:135–36).

5

IRRESISTIBLE GRACE

The Holy Spirit Supernaturally Calls the Elect

Called to a Holy Calling (2 Tim. 1:9)

If you have repented of your sin and received Christ, God has been inside your head.

All three persons of the Holy Trinity are involved in the salvation of sinners. We have seen the work of the Father in electing. Out of the entire human race, God the Father

> chose us in [Christ] before the foundation of the world, that we should be holy and blameless before him. In love he predestined us for adoption to himself as sons through Jesus Christ, according to the purpose of his will, to the praise of his glorious grace. (Eph. 1:4–6)

The Father gave these chosen ones to "our great God and Savior Jesus Christ, who gave himself for us to redeem us from all lawlessness and to purify for himself a people for his own possession who are zealous for good works" (Titus 2:13–14).

God the Son, then, has made certain that his people will be saved. He confidently asserted, "All that the Father gives me will come to me" (John 6:37).

When the elect are born into this world, however, though we are certainly destined for heaven, we are not yet ready to live there. Like the non-elect,

> You were dead in the trespasses and sins in which you once walked, following the course of this world, following the prince of the power of the air, the spirit that is now at work in the sons of disobedience—among whom we all once lived in the passions of our flesh, carrying out the desires of the body and the mind, and were by nature the children of wrath, like the rest of mankind. (Eph. 2:1–3)

By God's grace, heaven is in our future—but by nature, hell is in our hearts. If the Lord were to leave us in this sinful condition, even if we were to go to heaven we would not be happy there.

So the Lord changes us, and this is the work of the Holy Spirit. On the cross of his suffering, Jesus purchased salvation for us; now, from the throne of his glory, he applies salvation to us by his Holy Spirit. "God exalted him at his right hand as Leader and Savior, to give repentance to Israel and forgiveness of sins" (Acts 5:31). In offering up a particular redemption for his people, Christ purchased our ticket to heaven; in bestowing on us his irresistible grace, he makes us ready to live there. His atoning work does not actually save us until it is applied to us by his Holy Spirit. Christ spread a bountiful feast for sinners; the Holy Spirit leads us into the banqueting hall and enables us to sit down at the table and partake of the feast.

"Why was I made to hear Thy voice,
And enter while there's room,
When thousands make a wretched choice,
And rather starve than come?"

'Twas the same love that spread the feast
That sweetly forced us in;
Else we had still refused to taste,
And perished in our sin.[1]

Christ purchased our redemption, but we partake of it only when the Spirit effectively applies it to us by working faith in us and thereby uniting us to Christ in our effectual calling.[2] God the Father elected us; God the Son redeemed us; God the Holy Spirit calls us with an irresistible grace in our effectual calling.

God Must Intervene

In the chapter on Total Depravity, we saw why no one can come to Jesus unless the Father draws him. In this chapter we will explore how the Father draws those who do come—he *calls* them. But before we go any further, let Jesus's words recorded in John 6:44 sink in: "No one can come to me unless the Father who sent me draws him." God must do something to make a difference in the mind of anyone who comes to Jesus. Somehow, God so manages things that the elect always hear and obey his call. The sinner hears his call, welcomes his call, and obeys his call.

By nature, all sinners resist God's grace, but God

1. Isaac Watts, "How Sweet and Awful Is the Place," 1709.
2. See the Westminster Shorter Catechism, answers 29 and 30.

overcomes the resistance of his elect—and so we call it *irresistible grace*. God's call always produces the desired effect in the sinner, and so we say it is an effectual call. If you are a devoted follower of Jesus Christ, it is because God "called you out of darkness into his marvelous light" (1 Peter 2:9). At one time we "loved the darkness rather than the light" (John 3:19), but "he has delivered us from the domain of darkness and transferred us to the kingdom of his beloved Son" (Col. 1:13). Preaching "Christ crucified" may be "a stumbling block to Jews and folly to Gentiles, but to those who are called, both Jews and Greeks, [he is] Christ the power of God and the wisdom of God" (1 Cor. 1:23–24).

When a person repents of sin and believes in Christ, it is evidence that God has worked in the sinner so that he has stopped resisting God. He has been sweetly compelled by God's irresistible grace.

Irresistible?

When discussing the doctrine of irresistible grace, I prefer the phrase *effectual calling*, but the term *irresistible* is fine. When Jesus says, "No one can come to me unless the Father who sent me draws him," the word that is translated *draws* is quite a forceful Greek word. It appears only a few times in the New Testament, and usually the things being drawn are not necessarily cheerfully compliant with the drawing.[3] My point is that, similar to the word *irresistible*, the word that

---

3. In the following citations, the italicized word(s) are translations of the Greek word under consideration. Peter *drew* his sword (John 18:10); the disciples were not able *to haul in* the net full of fish (John 21:6, 11); they seized Paul and Silas and *dragged* them into the marketplace (Acts 16:19); they seized Paul and *dragged* him out of the temple (Acts 21:30); the rich are the ones who *drag* you into court (James 2:6).

Jesus uses for *draws* in John 6:44, while a metaphor, is a forceful metaphor.

Still, irresistible grace does not mean that God saves us against our wills. On the contrary, he makes us willing to comply with his grace. "It is God who works in you, both to will and to work for his good pleasure" (Phil. 2:13). "Your people will offer themselves freely on the day of your power" (Psalm 110:3). As a result of the Spirit's work, the elect freely repent of sin and believe in Christ. Like the Prodigal Son, we get sick of living in the pigsty and humbly go to the Father.

Bees and Honey

God is not at a loss for resources that he may use to make a person willing to comply with his plan. When we read about Israel's conquest of Canaan, it is easy to overlook a tiny warrior that God used to help Israel win their wars against the nations that had been living in Canaan. Naturally, those nations were not simply going to say, "Oh, your God is giving you this land? Okay. Here you go. We'll go live somewhere else." God used some very convincing little helpers to make the Canaanites eager to vacate the premises. "I will send hornets before you, which shall drive out the Hivites, the Canaanites, and the Hittites from before you" (Ex. 23:28). Hornets! A swarm of angry hornets will get your feet moving in a hurry.

I have been a beekeeper for nearly thirty years, and my father was a beekeeper when I was a child, so I have been around honeybees my entire life. When I work with my bees, I wear a protective veil to keep the bees from stinging me on my face, but I usually do not wear gloves, so I sometimes get stung a few times. Most beekeepers build up an immunity to honeybee venom, and I have as well—so, as incredible as it seems to non-beekeepers, I do not pay much attention to being stung five or six times on my hands. But, if I were not wearing any protective gear at all and I accidentally knocked over a beehive, I assure you I would immediately become willing to stop whatever I was doing and get out of there fast. When it comes to convincing humans to do his will, God has his hornets. He has his swarms of angry honeybees.

God also has his honey—the sweet, golden honey of his "kindness and forbearance and patience . . . [and] God's kindness is meant to lead you to repentance" (Rom. 2:4). He demonstrates over and over that he is "the LORD, the LORD, a God merciful and gracious, slow to anger, and abounding in steadfast love and faithfulness, keeping steadfast love for thousands, forgiving iniquity and transgression and sin" (Ex. 34:6–7).

The sight of such a God ought to make sinners rush to his throne of grace, joyfully shouting, "Who is a God like you, pardoning iniquity and passing over transgression for the remnant of his inheritance? He does not retain his anger forever, because he delights in steadfast love" (Mic. 7:18)—or, as this last phrase is translated in the King James Version, "he delighteth in mercy." He cheerfully invites sinners to "open your mouth wide, and I will fill it . . . with the finest of the wheat, and with honey from the rock" (Ps. 81:10, 16). God has his honey.

In spite of all God's bees and all his honey, "you refuse to come to me that you may have life" (John 6:40). The people of Jesus's day saw his wonderful miracles and heard his heavenly teaching, but they finally said, "We do not want this man to reign over us" (Luke 19:14). The bees of adversity and the honey of blessings may convince us to embrace Christian doctrine and even join a church, but when we realize that Jesus is a real, living person who insists on being absolute Lord of our lives, we agree with Jesus's contemporaries: "We do not want this man to reign over us." We agree with them, that is, until God makes us willing to change our minds.

Saved from Self-Destruction

God does not save us against our wills; but honestly, knowing what you know now, would it bother you if you found out that he had?

When one of my daughters was a toddler, she had no fear of water. Any time we were around water, we had to watch her carefully because she would just keep walking into deeper water until the waves were hitting her in the face. She would gasp and splutter, but she would not turn around. My wife and I would stare at each other in disbelief, thinking, *Surely she will learn her lesson*—but she would keep trudging into the deep water. We would pick her up and carry her to safety. Once she was safe in shallow water, she would immediately head back into the deep! I believe that she would have cooed and giggled into the deep water until she had done herself irreparable harm. She was out of her senses! Some might read this illustration and think that we were cruel and irresponsible to have let her go so far. "You ought to have snatched her from danger sooner!" No one thinks, *You ought to have let the stubborn little thing have her way.*

Looking back on my life before the Lord saved me, I was similar to my daughter in endangering myself. I was stupidly and gleefully marching into the depths of self-destructive sin. I was stumbling toward an eternity of separation from God. In spite of sometimes getting hit with waves of shame and conviction, I continued to trudge into ever deeper sin. I was on the brink of a drop-off that would have plunged me into an everlasting lake of fire. I was out of my senses! But God snatched me. "He drew me up from the pit of destruction, out of the miry bog, and set my feet upon a rock, making my steps secure" (Ps. 40:2). He did not do it against my will, but I would not mind if he had. I want God to do his will in my life even when I do not understand his will. Now that I am somewhat in my senses, I *ask* him to take over my mind and my affections and my will.

Before God called me, I did not want him to take over my life; and, as we saw in the chapter on Total Depravity, by nature no one wants God to take over his life. We all want to rule ourselves—to decide what is good and evil. So what changed my mind? Before my conversion, I loved sin and I hated God. Did I just wake up one morning and decide to reject the sin that I dearly loved and freely submit to the God who I earnestly hated? Of course not. I had to be changed, and God changed me. Jesus says that if God were to leave us alone, no one could come to him. The only way we will come to him is if the Father draws us.

Everyone Whom God Calls to Christ Comes to Christ

There is no way around it—just as I said earlier that you have got to believe something about *election* because it is in the Bible, so you have got to believe something about *drawing* or *calling* because it is in the Bible. It is not in only a few proof texts, either; calling is all over the Bible. Ten minutes with a Bible concordance will confirm that. If you believe the Bible, you have got to believe something about calling.

A Universal Call?

Of course, plenty of non-Calvinists believe the Bible. What do they believe about calling? Probably the most common theory is that, in some way, God calls everyone—that his call is *universal*. John 12:32 is often cited as proof of this, in which Jesus says, "And I, when I am lifted up from the earth, will draw all people to myself."

Jesus said, "I will draw all people to myself" on a specific occasion. Two of the disciples told him that there were some Greeks who wanted to see him, and this posed a problem since Jews did not freely fraternize with Greeks. Jesus prophesied that as the Savior of the world (and not of Jews only), he would draw persons from all people groups into his kingdom. In other words, the word *all* in this verse does not mean *all persons without exception*, but it means *all peoples without distinction*.[4] Whereas formerly God revealed himself to only one people group, the Jews, and he drew his saints almost exclusively from that one group, Jesus predicted a day when he would fling open the gates of mercy to the world and would draw saints to himself from all people groups. John 12:32 cannot legitimately be used to prove that God's effectual calling is directed to every human who has ever lived.

A further problem with the theory of universal calling is that the Bible teaches that those whom God effectually calls actually and infallibly come to Christ. In John 6, notice what Jesus says right after declaring that no one can come to him unless the Father draws him: "And I will raise him up on the last day" (v. 44). He continues, "It is written in the Prophets, 'And they will all be taught by God.' Everyone who has heard and learned from the Father comes to me" (v. 45).

Jesus says that on the last day he will raise those whom the Father draws, and it is clear from the context that he is raising them up to eternal life: "Whoever feeds on my flesh and drinks my blood has eternal life, and I will raise him up on the last day" (John 6:54). Furthermore, Jesus explains what it means for the Father to draw someone to him by quoting Isaiah 54:13: "They will all be taught by God" (John 6:45). He then asserts that everyone so taught by God comes to him.

---

4. Earlier in this book I have pointed out that the word *all* does not usually mean *everyone who has ever lived* (see pp. 104–7).

If God calls everyone, then everyone gets raised up to eternal life. Later in this chapter we will examine other Scriptures that teach that God's call is always effectual.

Meleagris Gallopavo

Another specious possibility is that God calls people, but that he ultimately leaves the decision up to each individual as to whether or not he or she comes to Jesus, and that this is as much as God ever does to call anyone. He does no more than this. This is what has been historically known as the *Meleagris gallopavo* theory—or, in English, the Wild Turkey theory. Okay, I made that up; but it makes for a good illustration.

In the spring, during the wild turkey mating season, male turkeys, or gobblers, will strut and gobble to impress the female turkeys, or hens. Normally, the hens will walk or fly to the gobblers, and the gobblers will not go to the hens. The gobbler waits for the hens to come to him. It is his nature to wait for the hens. The challenge of hunting a gobbler is that the hunter must work with the gobbler's desires and persuade him to do something that is contrary to his nature. The hunter makes a call that sounds like a hen, and then the hunter sits and waits for the gobbler to come. The hunter cannot go to the gobbler, because the gobbler has extremely keen eyesight, and he will see the hunter if he moves. The hunter has got to call the gobbler and coax him to come to the hen call.

Generally, the hunter is more intelligent than the gobbler, and he uses his superior intellect in an attempt to manipulate circumstances to his advantage. He wears camouflage to blend into the surrounding environment. He practices his calling so that he sounds like a hen. He determines how close he may approach the gobbler without spooking him, and he tries to make sure that there are no obstacles, such as a fence or a creek, between him and the gobbler.

When he "sets up" to call the gobbler, he may put out one or more decoys. A hunter increases his skill as he learns how to arrange everything to convince a gobbler to do something that is, on one level, unnatural to the gobbler. Sometimes the hunter is successful, but most of the time the turkeys do not heed the call.

Some people erroneously suppose that when God calls a sinner to himself, he does no more than the turkey hunter. Similar to the hunter, God knows how to arrange circumstances skillfully. He knows how to capitalize on our desires for love, for security, and for meaning in life so that we see that these desirable things are found only in him. He applies his skills of superior intellect, and then he sets up in a good hiding place to see if he can get a sinner to come in to him.

Before I show why this is an inadequate illustration of effectual calling, let me point out that while the "Wild Turkey theory" does not assign enough activity to God to be accurate, it does assign much! If you pray for God to save sinners, you surely must believe that God does at least as much when he calls sinners as a turkey hunter does when he calls to turkeys. You are asking him to arrange circumstances, bring significant people into the sinner's life, and make him dissatisfied with sin and with all the distractions that keep him occupied away from Christ.

But wait—are you praying that God will influence his thinking? A little bit or a lot? Are you praying that God will "get inside his head" and change him? Are you praying that God will change his basic fundamental affections? Are you praying that God will make him want Christ? Are you asking God to go so far as to plant thoughts, attitudes, and desires in him? How many? Just enough to "level the playing field," or enough to "tip the scales" in Jesus's favor? If this is the way you pray for God to work, then, at least when you are praying, you are way past the Wild Turkey theory of calling; you are well on your way to believing in effectual calling.

The General Call

The Bible teaches that God issues two different calls for sinners to repent of sin and believe in Christ. "Many are called, but few are chosen" (Matt. 22:14). In both calls, God summons humans to accept by faith the salvation that is provided in Christ. What I have described in the Wild Turkey theory has been termed by more sober-minded thinkers as the *General Call*.

In the preaching of the gospel, all sinners are invited to come to Christ. Jesus says, "Come to me, all who labor and are heavy laden, and I will give you rest" (Matt. 11:28). He really means it. The Lord says, "Turn to me and be saved, all the ends of the earth! For I am God, and there is no other" (Isa. 45:22). And he really means it. If a person refuses to hear and obey God's gracious call, it is his own fault and not God's. God *commands* all persons to repent and believe in Jesus: "He commands all people everywhere to repent" (Acts 17:30). "And this is his commandment, that we believe in the name of his Son Jesus Christ" (1 John 3:23). When a person refuses to obey the general call, he is persisting in his rebellion against God.

Characteristics of the General Call

The general call is a robust and earnest call to all humans. It is robust because the Lord plainly speaks his truth in various ways and because humans are capable of recognizing that God is speaking in these various ways. It is earnest because the Lord pleads passionately and sincerely when he calls all humans to repent of sin and trust in him. "O Jerusalem, Jerusalem, the city that kills the prophets and stones those who are sent to it!

How often would I have gathered your children together as a hen gathers her brood under her wings, and you were not willing!" (Matt. 23:37). The general call contains many gracious components that ought to be sufficient to effect the conversion of sinners, and it would be sufficient to convince anyone who was not already a determined rebel against God.

In the general call, which includes God's testimony in creation, God so thoroughly proclaims his character and human responsibility in the works of creation that all humans "are without excuse" (see Rom. 1:18–23). No one can say, "I had no idea that there was a God and that he expected anything of me." In the general call, God may orchestrate human events, "having determined allotted periods and the boundaries of their dwelling place, that they should seek God, and perhaps feel their way toward him and find him" (Acts 17:26–27).

God may unmistakably speak through the circumstances of life so that sinners are compelled to admit, "This is the finger of God" (Ex. 8:19) and even confess, "I have sinned; the LORD is in the right, and I and my people are in the wrong" (Ex. 9:27). God may speak through the reading and the preaching of his inspired Word as he did to the religious leaders who rejected Christ (see John 5:39–47). A person may be among those "who have once been enlightened, who have tasted the heavenly gift, and have shared in the Holy Spirit, and have tasted the goodness of the word of God and the powers of the age to come" (Heb. 6:4–5).

The general call is robust, and it is earnest.

The General Call Is Insufficient to Bring about Salvation

After all the gracious truths that are revealed and all the earnest motivations that are imbedded in the general call, the person who has heard only the general call will still refuse, if God does nothing more, to come to Jesus in simple faith for salvation. When a hunter calls to a gobbler, even though the turkey may be reluctant to come to the call, sometimes he stops resisting and comes to the caller. But based on the general call alone, sinful humans never make up their minds to stop resisting and go to the caller. God must do more than issue a general call. He must send his Holy Spirit to do a supernatural work in the heart of a sinner.

In doing this supernatural work, God must exert the same sort of power that he used when he created the world: "For God, who said, 'Let light shine out of darkness,' has shone in our hearts to give the light of the knowledge of the glory of God in the face of Jesus Christ" (2 Cor. 4:6). God is, in fact, making a new creation: "Therefore, if anyone is in Christ, he is a new creation" (2 Cor. 5:17). God does this when he bestows his irresistible grace on us in our effectual calling.

The Effectual Call

Effectual calling is the work of God's Spirit, whereby, convincing us of our sin and misery, enlightening our minds in the knowledge of Christ, and renewing our wills, he doth persuade and enable us to embrace Jesus Christ freely offered to us in the gospel.[5]

Effectual Calling Is the Work of God's Spirit

What the Holy Spirit does *in* us is as essential to our salvation as what Christ did *for* us.[6] Not only are the respective works of Christ and the Holy Spirit essential to our salvation, but both Christ and the Holy Spirit accomplish their respective

5. Westminster Shorter Catechism, answer 31.
6. See A. A. Hodge and J. A. Hodge, *The System of Theology Contained in the Westminster Shorter Catechism: Opened and Explained* (New York, 1888), 57.

works without our assistance. When Jesus died for us, there was nothing that we could to do help him or to add to his work. Similarly, when the Holy Spirit calls us, we do not help him or add to his work. To state it another way, while our resistance is broken down and we are not saved against our wills, we are nevertheless passive when the Holy Spirit makes us alive.

Consider again how the Lord describes our natural spiritual condition. We are dead in trespasses and sins (see Eph. 2:1; Col. 2:13). We are blind: "The god of this world has blinded the minds of the unbelievers, to keep them from seeing the light of the gospel of the glory of Christ, who is the image of God" (2 Cor. 4:4). Sinners are described as "darkened in their understanding, alienated from the life of God because of the ignorance that is in them, due to their hardness of heart" (Eph. 4:18). They are out of their senses, which can be inferred from the fact that when God grants repentance leading to a knowledge of the truth, they "come to their senses" (see 2 Tim. 2:25–26). By nature we are like a bad tree, and a bad tree bears only bad fruit (see Matt. 12:33–35). "The natural person does not accept the things of the Spirit of God, for they are folly to him, and he is not able to understand them because they are spiritually discerned" (1 Cor. 2:14). In such a state—dead, blind, and out of our senses—we cannot do what God requires of us. "Can the Ethiopian change his skin or the leopard his spots? Then also you can do good who are accustomed to do evil" (Jer. 13:23). If we are to be saved, only God can enable us to do what we must do.

A Significant Difficulty

When we begin to come to terms with the fact that the Holy Spirit must do a supernatural work in us before we can come to Christ, we encounter a significant mental difficulty. Besides the fact that we are naturally averse to the sovereignty of God, many modern persons have another difficulty to overcome: we do not really believe in the existence and activity of spirits, and for all practical purposes, that includes the Holy Spirit.

The ancient peoples saw spirits everywhere. In Greece and Rome, when an eagle or some other bird of prey appeared, they thought it to be a sign from the gods.

> Any occurrence which is not entirely a matter of course and which cannot be manipulated may become a sign: a sudden sneeze, a stumble, a twitch; a chance encounter or the sound of a name caught in passing; celestial phenomena such as lightning, comets, shooting stars, eclipses of sun and moon, even a drop of rain. . . . At Plataea, Greeks and Persians remained encamped opposite each other for ten days because the omens—obtained by the same techniques—did not advise either side to attack.[7]

It was not only pagans who saw spirits everywhere; early Christians also saw spirits and spiritual activity everywhere. Christians at Colossae were tempted to worship angels (see Col. 2:18), as were the early readers of the book of Hebrews. To counter this sinful obsession with angels, the Holy Spirit devotes the first two chapters of Hebrews (well over 10 percent of the book!) to demonstrating Christ's superiority over angels.

The ancient peoples saw spirits everywhere, but we cannot attribute their preoccupation with spirits entirely to sinful obsession; some of it was legitimate. Spirits are far more active and influential than many of us are willing to admit. With very little explanation, numerous biblical writers discuss the role

7. Walter Burkert, *Greek Religion* (Cambridge: Harvard University Press, 1985), 112–13.

of spirits in the cosmos, apparently even recognizing specific orders of spirit beings such as "rulers," "authorities," "powers," and others. For example, one of the primary functions of the gospel is "so that through the church the manifold wisdom of God might now be made known to the *rulers and authorities* in the heavenly places" (Eph. 3:10).

Apparently, some of these extraterrestrial rulers and authorities have the potential to harm us—for when describing the invulnerability of God's people, Paul writes,

> For I am sure that neither death nor life, nor *angels* nor *rulers*, nor things present nor things to come, nor *powers*, nor height nor depth, nor anything else in all creation, will be able to separate us from the love of God in Christ Jesus our Lord. (Rom. 8:38–39)

Through Jesus and his cross, God "disarmed the rulers and authorities and put them to open shame, by triumphing over them in him" (Col. 2: 15). In our fight for holiness, "we do not wrestle against flesh and blood, but against the rulers, against the authorities, against the cosmic powers over this present darkness, against the spiritual forces of evil in the heavenly places" (Eph. 6:12).

When we were dead in trespasses and sins, we were "following the prince of the power of the air, the spirit that is now at work in the sons of disobedience" (Eph. 2:2). According to Jesus, when some people hear the word of God, "the devil comes and takes away the word from their hearts, so that they may not believe and be saved" (Luke 8:12). Jesus said that those who wanted to kill him were acting like their father the devil (see John 8:37–38), and this also explained why they could not understand him: "Why do you not understand what I say? It is because you cannot bear to hear my word.

You are of your father the devil, and your will is to do your father's desires" (John 8:43–44). At the Last Supper, "the devil had already put it into the heart of Judas Iscariot, Simon's son, to betray him," and before the supper was ended, "Satan entered into him" (John 13:2, 27). As the time approached when Judas would betray him, Jesus said, "The ruler of this world is coming" (John 14:30).

If evil spirits possess such mind-controlling influence, why does it seem an incredible thing that the Holy Spirit of the living God possesses and exerts mind-controlling influence? Since the Evil Spirit can blind us, surely the Holy Spirit can give us sight. If the devil can put it into a man's heart to betray Jesus, surely the Holy Spirit can put it into a man's heart to receive Jesus.

The ancient peoples saw spirits everywhere, and perhaps they were often mistaken; but our mistake lies in the opposite extreme—we see spirits in nothing. We are the odd ones.

> The angels keep their ancient places,
> Turn but a stone and start a wing;
> 'Tis you, 'tis your estranged faces
> That miss the many splendored thing.[8]

Read a biography of Martin Luther, or read John Bunyan's spiritual autobiography, *Grace Abounding to the Chief of Sinners*, and you will be amazed at how real the devil was to these respected brothers. The complement to their keen awareness of the devil was their keen awareness of the Holy Spirit. If you do not believe in spiritual activity, then you will have weak

8. Francis Thompson, "The Kingdom of God," 1917. See also William Wordsworth's poem "The World Is Too Much with Us," in *Poems, in Two Volumes* (London, 1807), 1:122; and Maltbie D. Babcock's hymn, "This Is My Father's World," 1901.

notions of the Holy Spirit and the powerful way he works in the world. I fear that the approach of most twenty-first-century Christians is not far from the bleak, powerless expression of sympathy expressed by those who do not know God: "Our thoughts are with you." Formerly it was "Our thoughts and *prayers* are with you," but a blind honesty has prevailed and the superstitious *prayers* have been omitted. What good is prayer, anyway? Even for many Christians, belief in the Holy Spirit has been neatly tucked away into the same drawer of fantasy that contains trolls, fairies, and dragons.

To put it bluntly, there are unseen, nonhuman persons in our world, and they interact with humans. The third person of the Trinity is one of them. He is the most powerful of all spirits. He is the Spirit of Jesus Christ, and he is carrying on the work of Christ's kingdom. He is not a mere influence or force. He is not a religious state of mind, an attitude, a flavor of Christ, or the essential philosophy of Christianity. He is a person, and he has the ability to do everything that God does because he is God. He does what God alone can do. When God the Father works on earth, he works through the Holy Spirit. After he arose from the dead, Jesus went back to heaven, but he sent the Holy Spirit to carry on the work of the kingdom.

The Holy Spirit Does What God Alone Can Do

If we are to become partakers of the redemption purchased by Christ, we need the Holy Spirit to perform in us the supernatural, divine work that God alone can do, and that is what he does do when he effectually calls us to Christ. We cannot give birth to ourselves either physically or spiritually, yet "unless one is born again he cannot see the kingdom of God," and "unless one is born of water and the Spirit, he cannot enter the kingdom of God" (John 3:3, 5). A dead person cannot resurrect himself, but God, being rich in mercy, because of the great love with which he loved us, even when we were dead in our trespasses, *made us alive* together with Christ—by grace you have been saved—and *raised us up* with him. (Eph. 2:4–6)

We cannot create ourselves, but through the Spirit's work you are

to be renewed in the spirit of your minds, and to put on *the new self, created* after the likeness of God in true righteousness and holiness. (Eph. 4:23–24)

Therefore, if anyone is in Christ, he is *a new creation*. (2 Cor. 5:17)

In these Scripture passages, the Holy Spirit's work is described as giving birth, raising the dead, and creating a new person. These are acts in which the person acted on is passive, and the person doing the acting is performing acts that God alone can do.

One of Jesus's good friends, Lazarus, had died. Jesus never went to the grieving family until four days after Lazarus's death. The family and those who had come to console them were crying, but their tears could not bring Lazarus back to life. No doubt, at his funeral, someone spoke truth over his dead body, but Lazarus never stirred; he never heard. Oh, how they missed him and wished that he were still alive, but all their thoughts were powerless to move him to come back to them. He was dead.

But then Jesus stood outside the tomb, and "he cried out with a loud voice, 'Lazarus, come out,'" and a miraculous thing happened: "the man who had died came out" (John 11:43–44). It was one of Jesus's most powerful miracles, and it was so undeniably a divine work that many people believed in Jesus because of this miracle. The same evil men who were plotting to kill Jesus "made plans to put Lazarus to death as well, because on account of him many of the Jews were going away and believing in Jesus" (John 12:10–11).

As impressive as it was for Jesus to raise Lazarus from the dead, if we have eyes to see it, the Holy Spirit has been doing something even more impressive. He has been doing it for thousands of years, and he has done it millions of times: he raises spiritually dead people.

How does he do it? How did Jesus raise those who were physically dead? It does not help to say that he touched them or that he spoke to Lazarus. It is a mystery. He knew how to do it, and he did it. The evidence was undeniable. Lazarus was alive again.

So it is with the resurrection work in the hearts of spiritually dead humans. It is a mystery. The Holy Spirit knows how to do it, and he does it. The evidence is undeniable. Persons he has raised repent of sins they once cherished. They receive and rest on Jesus Christ alone for salvation. Haters of God become lovers of God. A process is commenced that results in sin-mangled humans being recreated in the image of God and set on a course that results in their obtaining the glory of Christ. "God chose you as the firstfruits to be saved, through sanctification by the Spirit and belief in the truth. To this he called you through our gospel, so that you may obtain the glory of our Lord Jesus Christ" (2 Thess. 2:13–14). We may not know how the Holy Spirit does his secret, mysterious work in us, but the Bible informs us of what he does and how we respond to his work.

The Holy Spirit Convinces Us of Our Sin and Misery

When the Lord Jesus promised to send us the Holy Spirit, he said, "When he comes, he will convict the world concerning sin . . . because they do not believe in me" (John 16:8–9). On the day of Pentecost, when the Holy Spirit was poured out, Peter preached a sermon about Jesus, proclaiming,

> "Let all the house of Israel therefore know for certain that God has made him both Lord and Christ, this Jesus whom you crucified."
> Now when they heard this they were cut to the heart, and said to Peter and the rest of the apostles, "Brothers, what shall we do?" (Acts 2:36–37)

That is a most telling sequence of events. The people who were *cut to the heart* by Peter's sermon were some of the same people who less than two months previous had been in the bloodthirsty crowd that was crying out, "Crucify him! Crucify him!" What happened? Why were they suddenly convicted about executing the man they had believed to be a blaspheming imposter? Did Peter move them with his eloquence? Did he give them facts about Jesus that they had never before considered? No. The Holy Spirit had come, and he convicted them of their sin. He cut them to the heart.

Before the convicting work of the Holy Spirit, a person may admit that he is a sinner, but his tendency will be to excuse his sin or dismiss it by saying, "Nobody's perfect." But in the effectual call, the sinner hears the Holy Spirit say, "These things you have done, and I have been silent; you thought that I was one like yourself. But now I rebuke you and lay the charge before you" (Ps. 50:21). The sinner responds,

> For I know my transgressions,
>   and my sin is ever before me.
> Against you, you only, have I sinned
>   and done what is evil in your sight,

so that you may be justified in your words
and blameless in your judgment. (Ps. 51:3–4)

Fear of God's righteous judgment is awakened in his heart like never before, and this fear contributes to the sense of misery that, perhaps for the first time, attends his conviction of sin. The awakened sinner cries out, "Because of sin I cannot have communion with God. I am under his wrath and curse. I am a participant in the rebellion that has brought sorrow and grief into this world. My sin has made me liable to all the miseries in this life, to death itself, and to the pains of hell forever."[9] He realizes that his problem is far deeper than the sins he has done—his very heart is corrupt with sin. What comes out of the faucet is dirty, because the pipes are corroded and the water source is polluted. All his supposed good works are seen to be nothing more than dressed-up sins, for he has done them all while marching in the army of Satan. "In our sins we have been a long time, and shall we be saved? We have all become like one who is unclean, and all our righteous deeds are like a polluted garment" (Isa. 64:5–6).

The Holy Spirit delivers us from the delusion that we are rich and prosperous and need nothing, and he convinces us that we are "wretched, pitiable, poor, blind, and naked" (Rev. 3:17).

The Holy Spirit Enlightens Our Minds in the Knowledge of Christ

Because of our sinfulness, we were blind to the glories of Christ. "He had no form or majesty that we should look at him, and no beauty that we should desire him" (Isa. 53:2). In addition to our being blinded by our own sinfulness, "the

9. See the Westminster Shorter Catechism, answer 19.

god of this world has blinded the minds of the unbelievers, to keep them from seeing the light of the gospel of the glory of Christ" (2 Cor. 4:4).

The Holy Spirit not only dispels satanic influence over us, he also sends the light into our darkness and opens our eyes to see. He shows us that Christ is *able* to save us. We see that Christ is a Savior who is exactly suited to our need. We are ignorant of God; the Holy Spirit reveals Christ to be a *prophet* who can teach us the will of God for our salvation. We are guilty of sin; the Holy Spirit reveals Christ to be a *priest* who has offered a sacrifice to satisfy divine justice and reconcile us to God. He is a priest who will take up our case and intercede for us before God. We are rebellious, proud, weak, and helpless; the Holy Spirit reveals Christ to be a *king* who can subdue us to himself, who can rule and defend us, and who can restrain and conquer all of his and our enemies.[10] Not only is Christ able to save us, the Holy Spirit also reveals that Christ is *willing* to save us. We hear Jesus say, "Whoever comes to me I will never cast out" (John 6:37). The confidence that Christ is willing to receive us is essential to our coming to him, "for whoever would draw near to God must believe that he exists and that he rewards those who seek him" (Heb. 11:6).

The Holy Spirit Renews Our Wills

The Holy Spirit renews our wills, and he persuades and enables us to embrace Jesus Christ, who is freely offered to us in the gospel. When the Holy Spirit convinces us of our sin and misery, and when he enlightens our minds in the knowledge of Christ, he is primarily working in our understanding and our affections. And he does more. He must do more, or

10. See the Westminster Shorter Catechism, questions 23–26.

we will never embrace Jesus Christ. He also must work on our will, "for the mind that is set on the flesh is hostile to God, for it does not submit to God's law; indeed, it cannot" (Rom. 8:7). What God did for Lydia, he must do for us: "The Lord opened her heart to pay attention to what was said by Paul" (Acts 16:14). When the Lord opens "the inner door of the will . . . the work is done, Christ and the sinner meet. It is the great work."[11] It is the great work of irresistible grace.

The Holy Spirit renews our wills. When humans became sinful, we essentially wanted something more than God. Anything that we put before God is an idol. Even if God were to forgive us of all our past sins, we would remain in rebellion against him unless our hearts were changed. We must be made into persons who want God more than we want anything or anyone else. He brings about this miraculous transformation in the new birth. Jesus said that unless a person is born of water and of the Spirit he will never enter the kingdom of God. When Jesus said this, he surely had in mind the promises of Ezekiel 36:25–27:

> I will sprinkle clean water on you, and you shall be clean from all your uncleannesses, and from all your idols I will cleanse you [this is being *born of water*]. And I will give you a new heart, and a new spirit I will put within you. And I will remove the heart of stone from your flesh and give you a heart of flesh. And I will put my Spirit within you, and cause you to walk in my statutes and be careful to obey my rules [this is being *born of the Spirit*].

11. Thomas Boston, *An Illustration of the Doctrines of the Christian Religion*, vol. 1 of *The Complete Works of the Late Rev. Thomas Boston, Ettrick: Including His Memoirs*, ed. Samuel M'Millan (1853; repr., Wheaton, IL: Richard Owen Roberts, 1980), 568.

When the Holy Spirit gives a person a heart of flesh, he has begun to restore that person to the healthy spiritual state that the Lord created humans to enjoy. In the new birth, the Lord does more than forgive sins. He does more than deliver us from hell. He restores his own image in us, giving us "the mind of Christ" (1 Cor. 2:16) and the Spirit of Christ: "Anyone who does not have the Spirit of Christ does not belong to him" (Rom. 8:9). He promises,

> I will put my laws into their minds,
>> and write them on their hearts,
> and I will be their God,
>> and they shall be my people.
> And they shall not teach, each one his neighbor
>> and each one his brother, saying, "Know the Lord,"
> for they shall all know me,
>> from the least of them to the greatest.
> For I will be merciful toward their iniquities,
>> and I will remember their sins no more. (Heb. 8:10–12,
>>> quoting Jer. 31:33–34)

Do you believe in Jesus? Do you freely choose to believe him and obey him? Why? When you believed, was it because you were more sensitive to spiritual ideas or were just a little smarter than the person who remains unrepentant and unbelieving? "Who sees anything different in you? What do you have that you did not receive? If then you received it, why do you boast as if you did not receive it?" (1 Cor. 4:7). Give credit where credit is due . . . no, credit is not enough—give worship where worship is due. "It is God who works in you, both to will and to work for his good pleasure" (Phil. 2:13). Think of it: if you have repented of sin and believed in Christ, God has been inside your head.

It gets even more astounding. If you have repented of sin and believed in Christ, not only has God been inside your head, he has stayed there.

Questions for Contemplation and Discussion

1. Ancient people, including Jesus and the Christians in the Bible, were keenly aware of the presence and activity of spirits in the world. Modern people, especially those who live in wealthy countries, are far less cognizant of spiritual activity in the world. Why? Is it the same in poor countries? Why?

2. When praying for unconverted loved ones, even non-Calvinists pray as if they believe in Irresistible Grace. Explain how and why.

3. When referring to the Holy Spirit, even confessing Trinitarians tend to use the pronoun *it*, rather than *he*, and to think of the Holy Spirit as a force rather than a person. Why?

4. Of the Five Points of Calvinism, Irresistible Grace is potentially the most offensive and frightening to the unconverted. Why?

5. In one sentence, can you summarize the doctrine of Irresistible Grace?

6

PERSEVERANCE
OF THE SAINTS

God Brings All His Children to Heaven

"I Give Them Eternal Life, and They Will Never Perish" (John 10:28)

During my college years and for a while afterward, I did a lot of hitchhiking. I would sometimes be on the road for several weeks at a time, and I travelled all over the United States. I was seeking adventure, but I was also on a mission. I witnessed to almost everyone who picked me up, and I shared the gospel with hundreds of people. When someone stopped to give me a ride, I would usually direct the conversation to the gospel as soon as I could, but there were times when I would wait. If I saw that the driver had religious books or literature in the car, I would wait to see whether he would initiate a gospel conversation. If he did not (and, sadly, he usually did not), then I would follow the example of our Lord when he appeared to the two disciples on the road to Emmaus: I would pretend to be ignorant—a role for which I am well suited—and I would introduce gospel conversation from the perspective of someone who was interested in becoming a Christian.

While hitchhiking on the West Virginia Turnpike, I got a ride with a man who was a preacher in a denomination that believes a saved person can lose his salvation. He was a friendly fellow, and I liked him a lot. As we rode along, we had two or three hours of conversation about the Bible and salvation, and during that time I was acting like a person who was seeking to know how to become a Christian. I got around to asking him, "So, if I become a follower of Jesus, can I ever lose my salvation?"

He said, "Yes, you can. You have got to confess your sins and ask for forgiveness every day."

I said, "Let me get this straight. If you and I were to get into a fuss, and you got sinfully angry with me, and then we had a wreck and you died before you asked the Lord to forgive you for your anger, you would go to hell for that sin?"

"Yes."

I said, "You know, I am not sure that I want a salvation like that. If my salvation ultimately depends on my keeping myself saved, I just do not see how I would ever make it to heaven."[1]

Is Salvation Your Work or Is It the Lord's Work?

"Salvation is of the LORD" (Jonah 2:9 KJV). From beginning to end, salvation is God's work. "Because of him you are in Christ Jesus, who became to us wisdom from God,

---

1. This was the gist of our conversation. When he pulled over to let me out, I told him that I was a devoted follower of Jesus. He said, "I thought you knew a lot about the Bible to be a lost man!"

righteousness and sanctification and redemption, so that, as it is written, 'Let the one who boasts, boast in the Lord'" (1 Cor. 1:30–31). The fact of the matter is, if you earned your salvation yourself, then you can lose it yourself. If, however, your salvation depends on the finished work of Jesus, then your salvation is eternally secure.

No believer is perfect, and a believer may sometimes fall into grievous sin. David did. Peter did. Yet, "though he fall, he shall not be cast headlong, for the Lord upholds his hand" (Ps. 37:24). False disciples may turn back and no longer walk with Jesus, but when Jesus asks one of his true disciples, "Do you want to go away as well?" that disciple answers, "Lord, to whom shall we go? You have the words of eternal life, and we have believed, and have come to know, that you are the Holy One of God" (John 6:67–69). Every one of those whom the Father elected, every one for whom Jesus died, every one whom the Holy Spirit calls will be glorified in heaven. "They are preserved forever" (Ps. 37:28), and God supplies each one with the grace to persevere to the end.

In *Pilgrim's Progress*, when Christian is in the House of the Interpreter, he sees a fire burning against a wall, and that fire represents the work of grace that is wrought in the heart of a believer. There is a man who is standing by the fire pouring water on it and trying to put it out, but the fire burns higher and hotter. Christian wonders what it means, and the Interpreter explains that the man trying to put out the fire is the Devil. Then he takes Christian to the other side of the wall,

> where he saw a man with a vessel of oil in his hand, of the which he did also continually cast, but secretly, into the fire.
> Then said Christian, What means this?
> The Interpreter answered, This is Christ, who continually, with the oil of His grace, maintains the work already

begun in the heart: by the means of which, notwithstanding what the devil can do, the souls of His people prove gracious still. And in that thou sawest that the man stood behind the wall to maintain the fire, that is to teach thee that it is hard for the tempted to see how this work of grace is maintained in the soul.[2]

Super-Christians?

Do you grant that there are some Christians in the world who are so committed to Christ that they cannot go back to living the way they lived before they began to follow Christ? Are there some Christians who have seen the vile nature of sin so clearly that a lifestyle of living in sin is repulsive to them, and who, even if they could enjoy the pleasures of sin and still go to heaven, would even then not choose a lifestyle of living in sin? Are there some Christians who believe so strongly in Jesus that they will never stop believing in him, never stop listening to him, and never stop following him? Are there some Christians who have been so influenced by Jesus that they have begun to think, feel, and act like Jesus? Are there such *super-Christians*?

There are such Christians—but they are not super-Christians; they are normal Christians. The Christians I have described are the only Christians who have repented of sin. They are the only Christians who have saving faith. They are the only Christians who have been made a new creation in Christ Jesus. These Christians will persevere to the end and live forever in heaven. The subject of this chapter is the

2. John Bunyan, *The Pilgrim's Progress from This World to That Which Is to Come*, in *The Works of John Bunyan*, vol. 3, *Allegorical, Figurative, and Symbolical*, ed. George Offor (1853; repr. Carlisle, PA: Banner of Truth, 1991), 100.

perseverance of *the saints*, not of the pseudo-saints. The Bible teaches the eternal security of *the believer*, not the eternal security of the hypocrite.

I suppose that everyone believes that when a person gets to heaven, he will be safe there. Satan can no longer deceive him. He will see the truth clearly: "For now we see in a mirror dimly, but then face to face. Now I know in part; then I shall know fully, even as I have been fully known" (1 Cor. 13:12). He will be delighted with God, and he will love the people who live in heaven. He will enjoy the activities that go on in heaven. He will have eternal life, and he will have a glorious nature. God will openly acknowledge him, and he will have no fear of judgment. After the resurrection, he will be perfectly blessed, both in soul and in body, in the full enjoyment of God through all eternity.[3] I suppose everyone believes this about eternal life in heaven.

The doctrine of the perseverance of the saints is rooted in the astounding teaching of the Bible that the kind of secure eternal life that everyone has in heaven commences on earth in every person who receives Christ as Lord and Savior. The saints in heaven may be happier than are the saints on earth, but they are not more secure.[4] Even now believers have eternal life: "For God so loved the world, that he gave his only Son, that whoever believes in him should not perish but have *eternal* life" (John 3:16). "Truly, truly, I say to you, whoever hears my word and believes him who sent me has eternal life. He does not come into judgment, but has passed from death to life" (John 5:24). In these Scriptures (and many more), Jesus promises eternal life to those who believe in him. Is it really

3. See the Baptist Catechism, answer 41; as well as the Westminster Shorter Catechism, answer 38.
4. See Augustus M. Toplady's hymn that begins, "A debtor to mercy alone."

eternal life if it can end? Logically it is not possible that the life Christ gives to believers is both *eternal* and at the same time *not eternal.*

The doctrine of the perseverance of the saints is the logical, biblical culmination of all that has been taught in the previous chapters of this book. Since God chose his people before the foundation of the world, and since Jesus has paid their ransom, and since the Holy Spirit has called them and made them holy, it stands to reason that "he who began a good work in you will bring it to completion at the day of Jesus Christ" (Phil. 1:6). The ultimate glorification of every believer is the final link in a golden chain of salvation that God himself forged in eternity past:

> For those whom he foreknew he also predestined to be conformed to the image of his Son, in order that he might be the firstborn among many brothers. And those whom he predestined he also called, and those whom he called he also justified, and those whom he justified he also glorified. (Rom. 8:29–30)

It just does not make sense that God would go to all the trouble and expense of doing all that he has done for the redemption of his elect and then not finish the job. "He who did not spare his own Son but gave him up for us all, how will he not also with him graciously give us all things?" (Rom. 8:32).

A Serious Misunderstanding

The doctrine of perseverance is like a golden crown that adorns the glorious body of God's sovereign grace. There are more than a few who would say that they believe only one of the Five Points of Calvinism, and the one they believe is this point—the perseverance or preservation of the saints. They want to hold to the crown while rejecting the body of sovereign grace that supports the crown. Such a position leaves the crown mysteriously floating in midair. I readily admit that these "one-point-Calvinists" have a substantial reason for holding so tenaciously to this one point: they see that it is taught in the Bible! They rightly take Jesus at his word when he says,

> My sheep hear my voice, and I know them, and they follow me. I give them eternal life, and they will never perish, and no one will snatch them out of my hand. My Father, who has given them to me, is greater than all, and no one is able to snatch them out of the Father's hand. I and the Father are one. (John 10:27–30)

The "one-pointers" at least know the meaning of *eternal*.

There is, however, a dangerous tendency that is inherent in holding to the crown of perseverance while rejecting the other four points. That dangerous tendency is hinted at in the name that the "one-pointers" often call this doctrine. Instead of referring to the doctrine as the *Perseverance of the Saints* or the *Eternal Security of the Believer*, they call it *Once Saved, Always Saved*.

Properly understood, there is nothing wrong with calling it that. It is catchy, memorable, and true. The real trouble is not what they call it, but the way they sometimes explain it. Regrettably, some of the one-pointers—not all, but some—who say that they believe in *Once Saved, Always Saved* have woefully deficient ideas of what it means for a person to be saved. For them, a person may "get saved" when he or she merely repeats "The Sinner's Prayer" (a prayer, by the way, that is not in the Bible). Or a person may "get saved" when he "walks down the aisle" (not in the Bible) or "asks Jesus into his heart" (also not in the Bible) or when she gets baptized. In brief, the person who "gets saved" has not necessarily repented. Perhaps the person has been told that all she need do is admit that she is a sinner—but merely admitting one's sin is not repentance.[5]

Repentance that leads to eternal life is a saving grace, and when a person repents, he has a true sense of his sin and has begun to see the mercy of God offered in Christ. He is grieved over sin, he hates sin, and he turns away from sin. At the same time, he turns to God fully intending to and trying to obey God.[6] Repentance is much more than admitting that I am a sinner! A superficial understanding of repentance leads to a superficial understanding of salvation.

Similarly, many of those who hold to *Once Saved, Always Saved* have a superficial understanding of saving faith. For them, faith in Jesus Christ may be no more than believing facts about Jesus or believing that Jesus died for sinners or even believing that "Jesus died for me." As noted in the chapter on Limited Atonement, nowhere does the Bible say that if you just believe that Jesus died for your sins you will be saved. You must receive the Christ who died for sinners and rose again from the dead. The fact that our church rolls are sometimes swollen with the names of people who give no evidence of spiritual life is a strong indication that we have often dealt with precious souls in a hurried, slipshod way. I am a Baptist, and we Baptists have historically stood for *believer's* baptism—but based on the disparity between the large number of inactive members on our church rolls and the members who faithfully

5. See C. H. Spurgeon's sermon "Confession of Sin—A Sermon with Seven Texts," in *New Park Street Pulpit* (London, 1858; repr., Pasadena, TX: Pilgrim Publications, 1981), 3:49–56, in which he examines the lives of seven men in the Bible who admitted, "I have sinned" but were not converted.

6. See the Westminster Shorter Catechism, answer 87.

attend our worship services, the evidence shows that we have settled for *consenter's* baptism. We will baptize anyone who consents to it. Consent to be baptized is not saving faith.

What, then, is saving faith? "Faith in Jesus Christ is a saving grace, whereby we receive and rest upon him alone for salvation, as he is offered to us in the gospel."[7] As I have mentioned earlier in this book, we are saved when we receive Christ—a person—and are not saved until we receive and rest upon him alone for salvation.

An Important Clarification

Some time ago, I was talking with a man who did not have long to live. He admitted that he was not ready to meet the Lord, and I was earnestly pleading with him to receive Christ. I explained the gospel to him as well as I could, but he seemed confused. He had lived long on the earth, but he had not used his days wisely. He knew little about Christ. After I left that day, I reflected on what I had told him, and I wondered, *What does he understand me to be saying when I tell him that he must receive Christ? What does he know about Christ? What if I were dying, and someone came and told me that in order to be ready to meet God, I had to receive Millard Fillmore? I cannot tell you five facts about Millard Fillmore, and my eternal salvation depends on receiving Millard Fillmore? If I read books about Millard Fillmore, and I learned a lot about him, and I believed what I learned, would that be the same thing as receiving him?*

Allow me to briefly explain what it means to receive Christ.

The word *Christ* means *anointed one*. It has become one of the names by which we refer to Jesus, but originally it was

7. Westminster Shorter Catechism, answer 86.

not a name but a title. Who is the Christ, or the *Anointed One*, and what does he do?

Under the old covenant, when God wanted to set a person aside to perform a special task, he would have one of his representatives pour oil on the person's head—anoint him—as a sign that he was the person God had chosen to do the job. There were three very important jobs, or *offices*, that God anointed select men to perform: that of (1) *prophet*, who spoke for God, (2) *high priest*, who offered sacrifices and interceded for the people, and (3) *king*, who conquered, defended, and ruled by God's authority.

As the *Christ*, or the *Anointed One*, Jesus has been authorized to do all three jobs—or to put it another way, he performs or *executes* all three offices. So when we receive Christ, we are receiving someone who is a prophet, a priest, and a king.

Christ executes the office of a *prophet* in revealing to us, by his Word and Spirit, the will of God for our salvation. Are you willing to receive Jesus as your prophet? Will you take his Word to be absolute truth and reject any ideas and philosophies that contradict his Word?

Christ executed the office of a *priest* in his offering up himself as a sacrifice to satisfy divine justice and to reconcile us to God, and he continues to execute it in making continual intercession for us. Are you willing to receive Jesus as your priest? It means that you must abandon any idea of saving yourself by your own good works. If you take Jesus to be your priest, then you will rely on him to represent you before God the Father and will trust him to do all that is necessary to make you right with God.

Christ executes the office of a *king* in subduing us to himself, in ruling and defending us, and in restraining and conquering all of his and our enemies. Will you receive Jesus as your king? Will you lay down your arms of rebellion, submit to his absolute rule, and look to him as your champion to deliver you from all your spiritual foes?

If you have received Jesus as your prophet, your priest, and your king, then you have received the Christ and are now a child of God.[8] When Jesus came to earth,

> He came to his own, and his own people did not receive him. But to all who did receive him, who believed in his name, he gave the right to become children of God, who were born, not of blood nor of the will of the flesh nor of the will of man, but of God. (John 1:11–13)

What a difference there is between believing something about the work of Christ and receiving Christ! We know who the true Christ is because of the true things that are said about him in the Bible—but do not confuse believing true things with receiving the true Christ.

Without Holiness, No One Will See the Lord

The problem with the doctrine of *Once Saved, Always Saved*, as it is held by many "one-point-Calvinists," is that it offers a false assurance of salvation to those who have never repented of sin or received Christ. A person who has "prayed the prayer" or "walked the aisle" or "asked Jesus into his heart" or been baptized is told that he has been eternally saved and that he must never allow Satan to cause him to doubt his salvation. This poor, deceived fellow may then live the rest of his life walking in darkness and in friendship with the world, never reading or hearing the warnings of the Bible that might

---

8. The ideas in this paragraph are summarized in the Westminster Shorter Catechism, questions 23–26.

alert him to his lost condition, such as "If we say we have fellowship with him while we walk in darkness, we lie and do not practice the truth" (1 John 1:6) and "You adulterous people! Do you not know that friendship with the world is enmity with God? Therefore whoever wishes to be a friend of the world makes himself an enemy of God" (James 4:4). The Lord Jesus said, "Not everyone who says to me, 'Lord, Lord,' will enter the kingdom of heaven, but the one who does the will of my Father who is in heaven" (Matt. 7:21).

Those who do not believe in the eternal security of the believer point the finger at those who hold to *Once Saved, Always Saved* and say, "You people believe that a man can get saved, spend the rest of his life as a drunkard, and still go to heaven when he dies!" Sadly, these finger-pointing critics are sometimes right, but that is not the teaching of the perseverance of the saints. Those of us who believe in Perseverance agree that all God's children must "strive for peace with everyone, and for the holiness without which no one will see the Lord" (Heb. 12:14).

The biblical doctrine of the perseverance of the saints is a far richer and more robust doctrine than what is often meant by *Once Saved, Always Saved*. The Bible teaches that God preserves believers by working faith in us and thereby permanently uniting us to Christ. In this way, believers are enabled to persevere to the end because of faith and because of union with Christ. In the words of the famous old hymn, Christ's atoning work cleanses us from the guilt of sin and also frees us from the power of sin:

> Rock of ages, cleft for me,
> Let me hide myself in thee;
> Let the water and the blood
> From thy riven side which flowed

Be of sin the double cure,
Cleanse me from its guilt and pow'r. [9]

Faith

What Faith Is Not

The nature of true saving faith ensures that believers will persevere to the end. Faith is not strong optimism. It is not the ability to imagine a desirable outcome and then convince yourself that the outcome you have imagined will certainly happen. I suspect that when the average person uses the word *faith*, he uses it as a synonym for *strong optimism*. For example, when a person is going through a trial, he might say, "But I know it is going to be all right, because I have faith." Faith in what?

When I was a young man, I had a dear friend who was a few years older than I. Before I knew him, my friend had been a healthy soldier in the United States Marines, until one night when he got into a fight in a bar and someone hit him over the head with a beer mug. He woke up several months later in a hospital room to find that he was a quadriplegic who had lost the ability to speak. He regained limited use of one arm, and he learned to speak haltingly, but he spent the rest of his life in a wheelchair in a nursing home. He gave glory to God for the incident, because God used his suffering to bring him to Christ. He always had a well-worn Bible on the tray in front of him, and he was a strong and faithful witness for the Lord.

But oh how my friend longed to be healed! In his final years, he fell under the influence of preachers on television who convinced him that if he only believed that he

9. Augustus Toplady, "Rock of Ages," 1794.

was already healed, then he would be healed. According to these preachers, if you believe that you are healed, then you must speak and act like it. During those final years when I would visit him, I would call him by name and ask him, "How are you?" In his slow, labored speech he would answer, "I'm healed." For many years now I trust that he has been rejoicing in the presence of God, but when he died, he left behind a quadriplegic body that was sown in weakness but will be raised in power. Faith may produce strong optimism, but faith is not strong optimism. A person may be strongly optimistic about something that is not true.

What Faith Is

"Faith is that persuasion of truth which is founded on testimony."[10] In other words, when you have faith, you believe something to be true merely because a person whom you judge to be trustworthy has said that it is true. In Christianity, God is the one who has testified to the essential ideas of our religion, and we have faith when we believe him.

At its most fundamental level, faith is believing what God has said. He is the God of truth, so we are safe in believing all that he reveals. The most important truths in life are not explained; they are revealed. We do not know these revealed truths because we have figured them out; we know them because we believe them. We believe them because God has spoken them. God has provided ample evidence that he has spoken in the Bible and that the Bible is therefore trustworthy. The experience of countless Christians confirms that the Bible is true and trustworthy. After God's ample attestation to the truthfulness of the Bible, if we insist that he further prove

10. A. A. Hodge and J. A. Hodge, *The System of Theology Contained in the Westminster Shorter Catechism: Opened and Explained* (New York, 1888), 121.

to us everything that he reveals there, we insult him, just as we would insult an honest man if we insisted that he provide proof for everything that he claimed to be true.[11]

I have sometimes heard preachers talk as if faith is the simplest, easiest thing in the world. They say that when you sit down in a chair, you believe that the chair will hold you up, and that this belief is faith. There may be some similarities between confidence in a chair and confidence in Christ, but the confidence in the chair is based on evidence and experience. God requires us to believe truth that is not fundamentally based on evidence and experience. While it is bolstered by evidence and experience, the ultimate reason for our belief in what he reveals is that he has said it and that we trust him.

Hebrews 11 begins with a description of faith: "Faith is the assurance of things hoped[12] for, the conviction of things not seen" (v. 1). The remainder of Hebrews 11 is filled with illustrations of saints who were commended for their faith. If you read that chapter, you will find that every person mentioned there did something courageous because he or she believed God, and that the only reason they had for acting

11. "Nothing can be more proud and vain than to believe no more than we can comprehend, or can make appear to be credible in itself. Is not this founding our faith on knowledge, and not on testimony? Is not this trusting God like a discredited witness in court, whose deposition is regarded only as it is collaterally supported? Is this honoring his wisdom or veracity? Is this receiving with meekness the engrafted word? Is this receiving the kingdom of heaven as a little child?" (William Jay, *Morning Exercises for Every Day in the Year* [repr., Harrisonburg, VA: Sprinkle Publications, 1998], 261–62).

12. Like faith, *hope* is often misunderstood. There are three essential components of Christian hope: (1) We believe a promise that God has made for the future. (2) We are happy about the promise, and we want God to fulfill it. (3) We cooperate with the means that God has ordained for the accomplishment of the promise.

courageously was because God had revealed truth to them. In most cases, evidence and experience would have led them to disobey God, but they did what they did because they saw "him who is invisible" (v. 27). Faith is the way that we see the invisible and the way that we know the unknowable.

Faith Is a Legitimate Means of Knowing

In the twenty-first century, we have grown accustomed to the idea that everything worth knowing can be proven empirically—that is, that all truth can be discovered through scientific observation and experimentation or can be proven mathematically or can be demonstrated to be inarguably true through logic. According to this pervasive idea, everything that cannot be proven empirically is mere opinion. We are told, "What is in the Bible may be true for you, but it cannot be proven. It is only a matter of opinion, and therefore it cannot be True."

It is stunning and disheartening how many Christians have shrugged their shoulders, smiled an embarrassed little smile, and acceded to this fundamentally indefensible worldview. Some have even submitted the truths of the Bible to this worldly litmus test—but "those whom the Holy Spirit has inwardly taught truly rest upon Scripture, and that Scripture indeed is self-authenticated; hence, it is not right to subject it to proof and reasoning. And the certainty it deserves with us, it attains by the testimony of the Spirit."[13] The most important truths in the world cannot be proven empirically. For example, it cannot be proven that reason is a reliable means of recognizing truth. It is a reliable means, but this cannot be

13. John Calvin, *The Institutes of the Christian Religion*, ed. John T. McNeill, trans. Ford Lewis Battles (Philadelphia: Westminster Press, 1960), 1.8.5.

proven—especially if the attempt is made from a purely naturalistic standpoint.[14]

When the giver of testimony is trustworthy, faith is a legitimate means of knowing. This is certainly the case when we receive God's testimony by faith. We attain a sort of knowledge that is impossible apart from faith.

> When we call faith "knowledge" we do not mean comprehension of the sort that is commonly concerned with those things which fall under human sense perception. For faith is so far above sense that man's mind has to go beyond and rise above itself in order to attain it. Even where the mind has attained, it does not comprehend what it feels. But while it is persuaded of what it does not grasp, by the very certainty of its persuasion it understands more than if it perceived anything human by its own capacity. Paul, therefore, beautifully describes it as the power "to comprehend . . . what is the breadth and length and depth and height, and to know the love of Christ, which surpasses knowledge" [Eph. 3:18–19].[15]

Faith Is Not a Work

Since "in the wisdom of God, the world did not know God through wisdom" (1 Cor. 1:21), faith is the only possible means of knowing God, and "without faith it is impossible to please him" (Heb. 11:6). The complement to this is that

---

14. In his book *Miracles*, C. S. Lewis shows that pure Naturalism cannot account for human reason, and that human reason is evidence that we are not living in a closed system. He makes the same point regarding the universal standards of human morality (C. S. Lewis, *Miracles* [New York: Macmillan, 1947]; see esp. chap. 3, "The Self-Contradiction of the Naturalist," and chap. 5, "A Further Difficulty in Naturalism").

15. Calvin, *Institutes*, trans. Battles, 3.2.14.

with faith it is possible to please God. While faith, *per se,* is a human response, and therefore not a supernatural act, no human ever exercises saving faith apart from the supernatural work of God in him.[16]

> For by grace you have been saved through faith. *And this is not your own doing; it is the gift of God,* not a result of works, so that no one may boast. (Eph. 2:8–9)

Faith is a condition of salvation, but faith is not a work. On the contrary, faith entails the cessation of works that might otherwise be performed in the hope of earning salvation. Faith may be compared to a hole that is dug to receive a tree seedling. The hole is necessary, but the tree is the living, growing thing. The hole is empty; it is nothing. Again, faith is like a bandage that is used to apply a healing medicine to a wound. The bandage is not the medicine, but it is necessary to keep the medicine on the wound. The Bible says that we are saved by faith, but that does not mean that faith itself saves us. It is the one in whom we have faith who saves us.

Before I understood this, I was constantly examining myself, asking, "Have I believed enough? Is my faith strong enough?" I finally came to realize that it was not the size of my faith that saved me; it was the Savior I believed in who saved me. If my faith is no larger than a grain of mustard seed but is sown in the good soil of Christ, it is saving faith. A man is never more of a man than when he has faith in Jesus, but faith is a passive virtue—faith receives truth. The receptive nature of faith is reflected in the fact that the church is called the bride of Christ. We submit to him; we respond to him. Christ is like the sun; faith is like the moon that receives all

---

16. This is explained at length in chapter 5, "Irresistible Grace."

her glory from the sun. Faith is not a work, but saving faith is always accompanied by works. "What good is it, my brothers, if someone says he has faith but does not have works? Can that faith save him? . . . Faith by itself, if it does not have works, is dead" (James 2:14, 17).

Works That Accompany Faith

While it is impossible for one of God's elect to finally become lost and perish, it is possible for us to be deceived about someone's salvation, and it is possible for a person to be deceived about his own salvation.

> Therefore, brothers, be all the more diligent to confirm your calling and election. (2 Peter 1:10)

> Every healthy tree bears good fruit, but the diseased tree bears bad fruit. A healthy tree cannot bear bad fruit, nor can a diseased tree bear good fruit. Every tree that does not bear good fruit is cut down and thrown into the fire. Thus you will recognize them by their fruits. (Matt. 7:17–20)

The Holy Spirit has identified many fruits, or evidences, that will help us to honestly discern whether we have saving faith. When we see these scriptural evidences in our hearts and lives, then "the Spirit himself bears witness with our spirit that we are children of God, and if children, then heirs—heirs of God and fellow heirs with Christ" (Rom. 8:16–17).

The Holy Spirit bears witness most unmistakably in the written Word, not in some undefined sense of well-being that might embolden us to say, "I just know that I know." So let us measure ourselves by the evidences of God's Word. Furthermore, do not let Freudian psychology give you either false hope or unnecessary fears. The inadvertent self is not the real you; the self that you deliberately cultivate and nurture in secret is the real you. There is nothing hidden that will not be made known. What is in the heart will eventually come out. "Out of the abundance of the heart the mouth speaks. The good person out of his good treasure brings forth good, and the evil person out of his evil treasure brings forth evil" (Matt. 12:34–35).

When the Holy Spirit indwells a person, he makes his presence known by producing good fruit in that person's life. "The fruit of the Spirit is love, joy, peace, patience, kindness, goodness, faithfulness, gentleness, self-control" (Gal. 5:22–23). A person who does not bear the fruits of the Spirit does not have the Spirit. "Anyone who does not have the Spirit of Christ does not belong to him" (Rom. 8:9).

The Word of God is filled with evidences and examples of godly character, but the little book of 1 John was written specifically to identify and confirm true, saving faith: "I write these things to you who believe in the name of the Son of God, that you may know that you have eternal life" (1 John 5:13). The entire book of 1 John describes genuine faith and Christian character, but let us notice six of the outstanding marks of a true Christian that are described in the book.

True believers have stopped walking in the darkness of sin, and they are walking in the light of God.

> God is light, and in him is no darkness at all. If we say we have fellowship with him while we walk in darkness, we lie and do not practice the truth. But if we walk in the light, as he is in the light, we have fellowship with one another, and the blood of Jesus his Son cleanses us from all sin. (1:5–7)

True believers keep Christ's commandments and practice righteousness.

> Whoever says "I know him" but does not keep his com-
> mandments is a liar, and the truth is not in him, but who-
> ever keeps his word, in him truly the love of God is per-
> fected. By this we may know that we are in him: whoever
> says he abides in him ought to walk in the same way in
> which he walked. . . .
>
> If you know that he is righteous, you may be sure that
> everyone who practices righteousness has been born of
> him. (2:4–6; 29; see also John 14:15, 23–24)

True believers love other believers.

> Whoever says he is in the light and hates his brother is still
> in darkness. Whoever loves his brother abides in the light,
> and in him there is no cause for stumbling. (2:9–10)

> We know that we have passed out of death into life,
> because we love the brothers. (3:14; see also 4:7–8)

*True believers do not love the world—the system that finds its joy
outside of God.*

> Do not love the world or the things in the world. If anyone
> loves the world, the love of the Father is not in him. For all
> that is in the world—the desires of the flesh and the desires
> of the eyes and pride of life—is not from the Father but is
> from the world. (2:15–16)

True believers do not keep practicing a lifestyle of sin.

> No one who abides in him keeps on sinning; no one who
> keeps on sinning has either seen him or known him. Little

children, let no one deceive you. Whoever practices righteousness is righteous, as he is righteous. Whoever makes a practice of sinning is of the devil, for the devil has been sinning from the beginning. The reason the Son of God appeared was to destroy the works of the devil. No one born of God makes a practice of sinning, for God's seed abides in him; and he cannot keep on sinning, because he has been born of God. By this it is evident who are the children of God, and who are the children of the devil: whoever does not practice righteousness is not of God, nor is the one who does not love his brother. (3:6–10; see also 5:18)

True believers believe that Jesus is the Christ.

Everyone who believes that Jesus is the Christ has been born of God. (5:1)

Saving Faith Endures

Sometimes there are persons who demonstrate some of the evidences of true faith for a while, but like the seed sown among thorns or on rocky soil, they do not endure (see Luke 8:13–14). When such persons fail to persevere, they simply show that whatever faith they might have had was not true saving faith. "They went out from us, but they were not of us; for if they had been of us, they would have continued with us. But they went out, that it might become plain that they all are not of us" (1 John 2:19). Salvation is not promised to temporary believers; it is promised to believers who continue in the faith.

And you, who once were alienated and hostile in mind, doing evil deeds, he has now reconciled in his body of flesh by his death, in order to present you holy and blameless and above reproach before him, *if indeed you continue in the faith*, stable and steadfast, not shifting from the hope of the gospel that you heard. (Col. 1:21–23)

There are many Scriptures that identify true faith as faith that endures to the end.

We have come to share in Christ, if indeed we hold our original confidence firm to the end. (Heb. 3:14)

The one who endures to the end will be saved. (Mark 13:13)

Union with Christ

In our effectual calling, the Holy Spirit works faith in us and thereby unites us to Christ. We are in Christ, and Christ is in us. "Whoever keeps his commandments abides in him, and he in him. And by this we know that he abides in us, by the Spirit whom he has given us" (1 John 3:24, alternative text in footnote). Our union with Christ ensures that every true believer will persevere to the end. The Bible teaches that when a person receives Christ, Christ and that person become one. The believer is now *in Christ*.

And because of him you are in Christ Jesus, who became to us wisdom from God, righteousness and sanctification and redemption, so that, as it is written, "Let the one who boasts, boast in the Lord." (1 Cor. 1:30–31)

God has seen fit to deal with human beings through representative heads. There have been two representative heads: the first man, Adam, and the Lord Jesus, who is called "the last Adam" (1 Cor. 15:45). Before being united to Christ we were *in Adam*. "For as in Adam all die, so also in Christ shall all be made alive" (1 Cor. 15:22). When we were in Adam, we were represented by Adam, and our nature was changed by the consequences of his disobedience. Now that we are in Christ, we are represented by Christ, and our nature has been changed by the consequences of his obedience.

> Therefore, as one trespass led to condemnation for all men, so one act of righteousness leads to justification and life for all men. For as by the one man's disobedience the many were made sinners, so by the one man's obedience the many will be made righteous. (Rom. 5:18–19)

Every human being is either in Adam or in Christ. One need do nothing to be in Adam; simply being born a human in the ordinary way means that we are originally represented by Adam, the first man. The inevitable consequences of Adam's disobedience have been explained in the chapter on Total Depravity. To be in Christ, one must be born again and believe in Christ. When we are united to Christ, there are definite benefits that are credited to us because of Christ's obedience. Christ is the one who obeyed, but God treats us as if we had obeyed. That is, Christ works *for* us. We are justified and adopted.

At the same time, when we are united to Christ, there are benefits that are produced in us. He influences the way that we think and act so that we are changed to look like him. That is, Christ works *in* us. We are sanctified. What Christ does *for* us ensures that no one united to Christ can ever be damned. What Christ does *in* us ensures that everyone united to Christ will persevere to the end.

What Christ Secures for Us

Justification

"Justification is an act of God's free grace, wherein he pardons all our sins, and accepts us as righteous in his sight, only for the righteousness of Christ imputed to us, and received by faith alone."[17] In justification, the verdict of God's eternal judgment is pronounced at the moment a person believes in Christ. That verdict is "Not guilty." He pardons all our sins. "Through this man forgiveness of sins is proclaimed to you, and by him everyone who believes is freed from everything from which you could not be freed by the law of Moses" (Acts 13:38–39).

All your sins are pardoned. Has it ever occurred to you that when Christ died for your sins, all your sins were future? When God justifies a sinner, he applies a remedy that covers all that person's sins—past, present, and future. If a believer could lose his salvation, it would be because of sins committed after his conversion, but all those "post-conversion sins" were paid for in Christ's atoning work accomplished long ago on the cross. God harbors no more wrath against those who believe in Christ, for his wrath against them has been satisfied by Christ's propitiatory sacrifice. Believers still pray, "Forgive us our debts as we forgive our debtors," but the debts that we owe are debts owed to a loving Father, not those owed to an angry Judge. He has pardoned all our sins.

> From whence this fear and unbelief?
> Hast thou, O Father, put to grief
> Thy spotless Son for me?
> And will the righteous Judge of men

17. Westminster Shorter Catechism, answer 33.

Condemn me for that debt of sin
Which, Lord, was charged on thee?

Complete atonement thou hast made,
And to the utmost farthing paid
Whate'er thy people owed;
How then can wrath on me take place,
If sheltered in thy righteousness,
And sprinkled with thy blood?

If thou has my discharge procured,
And freely in my room endured
The whole of wrath divine,
Payment God cannot twice demand,
First at my bleeding Surety's hand
And then again at mine.

Turn then, my soul, unto thy rest;
The merits of thy great High Priest
Speak peace and liberty;
Trust in his efficacious blood,
Nor fear thy banishment from God
Since Jesus died for thee.[18]

You are accepted as righteous. As marvelous as it is that he has
pardoned all our sins, pardon for sin is only half of what
God does for us when he justifies us. He also accepts us as
righteous in his sight, because of the righteousness of Christ
imputed to us. Look at this number line:

-10 -9 -8 -7 -6 -5 -4 -3 -2 -1 0 1 2 3 4 5 6 7 8 9 10

18. Augustus Toplady, "From Whence This Fear and Unbelief," 1772.

Let all the numbers on the negative side of zero represent sinfulness. All humans in Adam fall somewhere on the negative side. Some persons are very wicked (maybe a negative 10), and others are less wicked (maybe a negative 1 or a negative 2). But everyone is on the negative side, for everyone is a sinner. Adam started out on the positive side of zero, but he fell into sin and "the covenant being made with Adam, not only for himself, but for his posterity, all mankind, descending from him, by ordinary generation, sinned in him, and fell with him, in his first transgression."[19]

Let the numbers on the positive side represent righteousness. Only one human has ever lived his entire life on the positive side. Jesus lived his entire life on the positive side, and he lived a perfect 10! He not only avoided all sin, he always did what God wanted him to do. He was perfectly righteous.

When God pardons all our sins, he brings us up to zero; all our sins represented by the negative numbers are wiped out and forgotten. But then God does an amazingly gracious thing—he credits us with the righteousness of Christ. The righteousness he lived out as a human being is given to us, and God treats us as if we were the ones who were perfectly righteous. Christ Jesus becomes to us righteousness (see 1 Cor. 1:30).

> Therefore, since we have been justified by faith, we have peace with God through our Lord Jesus Christ. Through him we have also obtained access by faith into this grace in which we stand, and we rejoice in hope of the glory of God. (Rom. 5:1–2)

We can't lose our salvation. We are eternally secure, because Christ paid the penalty for our sins and God has pardoned us.

19. Westminster Shorter Catechism, answer 16.

Beyond that, we have also been credited with the righteousness of Christ, and that righteousness cannot be diminished. God accepts us because of what Christ has done for us. If salvation were based on our righteousness, we might lose our salvation—but since it is based on Christ's righteousness, we can never lose our salvation.

This righteousness is received by faith alone. Not faith plus works—faith alone. It could not be faith plus works, because works performed for salvation displace faith.

> To the one who does not work but believes in him who justifies the ungodly, his faith is counted as righteousness, just as David also speaks of the blessing of the one to whom God counts righteousness apart from works:
>
> > "Blessed are those whose lawless deeds are forgiven,
> >   and whose sins are covered;
> > blessed is the man against whom the Lord will not
> >   count his sin." (Rom. 4:5–8)

> We know that a person is not justified by works of the law but through faith in Jesus Christ, so we also have believed in Christ Jesus, in order to be justified by faith in Christ and not by works of the law, because by works of the law no one will be justified. (Gal. 2: 16)

As proven above, the faith by which we are justified is a gift of God, and it will endure. Therefore, believers are eternally secure.

Adoption

"Adoption is an act of God's free grace, whereby we are received into the number, and have a right to all the privileges of the sons of God."[20] All those who receive Christ are adopted into God's family.

> To all who did receive him, who believed in his name, he gave the right to become children of God. (John 1:12)

> See what kind of love the Father has given to us, that we should be called children of God; and so we are. (1 John 3:1)

I have known couples who have waited years and invested thousands of dollars to adopt a child into their family. Our adoption into God's family cost him dearly. He waited until the exact right time.

> But when the fullness of time had come, God sent forth his Son, born of woman, born under the law, to redeem those who were under the law, so that we might receive adoption as sons. And because you are sons, God has sent the Spirit of his Son into our hearts, crying, "Abba! Father!" So you are no longer a slave, but a son, and if a son, then an heir through God. (Gal. 4:4–7)

Note the certain connection between being a son and receiving the inheritance. "The slave does not remain in the house forever; the son remains forever" (John 8:35). If you are a son, then you are in God's family forever and will receive the promised inheritance.

> Blessed be the God and Father of our Lord Jesus Christ! According to his great mercy, he has caused us to be born again to a living hope through the resurrection of Jesus

20. Westminster Shorter Catechism, answer 34.

Christ from the dead, to an inheritance that is imperishable, undefiled, and unfading, kept in heaven for you, who by God's power are being guarded through faith for a salvation ready to be revealed in the last time. (1 Peter 1:3–5)

God's own integrity is bound up in the salvation of his children. He would be dishonored if any were lost, and he rightly receives all glory for our salvation. When we believed in Christ, we "were sealed with the promised Holy Spirit, who is the guarantee of our inheritance until we acquire possession of it, to the praise of his glory" (Eph. 1:13–14).

Results of Christ's Work in Us

He Gives Us the Heart of a Child

In a couple of my favorite hymns, Isaac Watts refers to humans using a most unflattering word. Here is a stanza from the first hymn:

> Alas! and did my Saviour bleed,
>   and did my Sovereign die!
> Would he devote that sacred head
>   for such a worm as I![21]

Here is a stanza from the second:

> A guilty, weak, and helpless worm,
>   On thy kind arms I fall;
> Be thou my strength and righteousness,
>   My *Jesus*, and my all.[22]

21. Isaac Watts, "Alas! And Did My Savior Bleed," 1707.
22. Isaac Watts, "How Sad Our State by Nature Is!" 1709.

In case you didn't notice, the unflattering word is *worm*. As I said, these stanzas are taken from two of my favorite hymns, and I think that Watts chose his words wisely. In both hymns, he describes the meditations of a person who is in the process of coming to Christ, and that person is acknowledging his own sinfulness and unworthiness. There is a time for thinking of ourselves in terms as lowly as possible, and a worm is pretty low.

There are a few times in the Bible when the Holy Spirit guided the writer to use the word *worm* to describe humans, but no biblical writer ever calls a saved person a *worm*. What we are called, as noted in the section immediately before this one, is *children of God*. And we are not merely *called* children of God—"so we are" (1 John 3:1). "To be a child of God, is a figurative expression, descriptive of intimate and peculiar relation to God, and of moral conformity and resemblance to God. . . . The clearest evidence of individuals being the children of God, the objects of his peculiar love, is their possession of those holy dispositions which he alone can confer, and which he confers only on those whom it is his purpose to bless with final salvation."[23]

After we are adopted into God's family, we are not perfect. Oh, no—far from it. We still have the desires of the flesh, so we must heed the exhortation of the Lord, who tells us, "Walk by the Spirit, and you will not gratify the desires of the flesh. For the desires of the flesh are against the Spirit, and the desires of the Spirit are against the flesh, for these are opposed to each other, to keep you from doing the things you want to do" (Gal. 5:16–17). The struggle for holiness is fierce. The Christian life commences in resting, but it progresses in wrestling.

23. John Brown, *Discourses and Sayings of Our Lord* (1852; repr., Carlisle, PA: Banner of Truth, 1990), 1:141–42.

We Are Not Alone

In this ongoing struggle, however, I fear that many Christians have never recognized and embraced the ongoing implications of Irresistible Grace. We humbly acknowledge that God must do a supernatural work in us to enable us to embrace Jesus Christ, but the manner in which we subsequently talk about ourselves seems to indicate that we believe that the Holy Spirit becomes dormant in us after conversion. If you believe in Jesus, God has been *inside your head*, yes—but do not stop there. One of the primary ways that God enables you to persevere in faithfulness to Christ is that he *stays inside your head*. "If anyone loves me, he will keep my word, and my Father will love him, and we will come to him and make our home with him" (John 14:23). When you receive Christ, God moves in with you. When we were totally depraved, we could not come to Christ because we did not want to come to him. Now that we have been born again, we stay faithful to Christ because we want to stay with him.

We Are Loved

I often hear this Scripture read as a benediction: "Now may the God of peace who brought again from the dead our Lord Jesus, the great shepherd of the sheep, by the blood of the eternal covenant, equip you with everything good that you may do his will, working in us that which is pleasing in his sight, through Jesus Christ" (Heb. 13:20–21). Does God ever answer that prayer? Does he ever equip us with everything good that we may do his will? Does he work in us that which is pleasing in his sight? Is he pleased with us?

I get the impression from a lot of Calvinistic preaching that God really does not like anyone but Jesus. Oh, he loves us, it is granted, but it is no more than a benevolent love. He loves us only because of the good person that he plans to make us one day—but today! . . . he can barely stand to have us around him. That is not true. God does love us benevolently, yes. That is the only way he could love us when he loved us in eternity past and up until our conversion. But when he reconciled us to himself, he was reconciled to us and we were reconciled to him, and he loves us not only for what he is going to make of us one day but because of what he has made us today: his children. If you are a believer, you are part of a noble family headed by a Father who loves you.

We Can Please God

When I was a boy living at home, often when I was heading out the door, my father would say to me, "Son, don't forget that you are an Orrick." There was a lot behind that short admonition. He was saying, "Son, our family has a good reputation in this community. People know that we are Christians. They know that you are the son of the Baptist pastor. Conduct yourself with honor. It takes a lifetime to build up a good name, but it can be destroyed in a moment. Do not forget who you are. You are an Orrick."

Christian, hear your heavenly Father admonishing you as you head out the door each day: "Child, don't forget that you are a son of God. Whatever comes your way today, show the world how a son of God behaves." There is motivation toward perseverance in that.

There is also great motivation toward righteous living when you know that you can actually please your Father and bring glory to him by the good works that you do. I played basketball and ran track throughout high school and college. I had some coaches who seemingly could not be pleased. If we were losing a game, one coach would call a time out and threaten us, "Boys, if you lose this game, we'll go back to the gym and I'll run you until midnight!" The threat of punishment is not entirely ineffective, but the incentive of reward and the power of approval are much more effective. I had a few coaches who recognized the power of encouragement. When one of those coaches said, "Good hustle!" or "Great effort!" it did not make us lazy. The fact that he was pleased with us motivated us to give our best effort again.

> Let your light shine before others, so that they may see your good works and give glory to your Father who is in heaven. (Matt. 5:16)

> Your Father who sees in secret will reward you. (Matt. 6:4, 6, 18)

> God is not unjust so as to overlook your work and the love that you have shown for his name in serving the saints, as you still do. (Heb. 6:10)

Those who do well will one day hear God say, "Well done!"— and even now, he is pleased with you. Everything good in us is the result of his grace, but he is pleased when we freely give it to him.

When my children were little and had no money, I would give them money to buy a Christmas present or a birthday present for me. Even though the gift was purchased with my money, it was still precious to me because my children gave it to me in love.

We Are Being Sanctified

When God moves in with you, he changes you. He transforms you into a person he likes. He sanctifies you. "Sanctification is the work of God's free grace, whereby we are renewed in the whole man after the image of God, and are enabled more and more to die unto sin, and live unto righ-teousness."[24]

In the chapter on Total Depravity, I explained how the fall adversely affected every aspect of human nature: our understanding was darkened, our affections were corrupted, and our will was perverted. Not only that, but human nature got turned upside down so that we were no longer ruled by understanding; instead, our affections began to rule. All that topsy-turvy mess eventually gets fixed in sanctification. It does not get fixed all at once, and it is not perfectly fixed until we get to heaven; but beginning at our conversion, we are enabled more and more to die unto sin and live unto righ-teousness.

Before conversion, the things of the Spirit of God were folly to us; but following conversion, "we have the mind of Christ" (see 1 Cor. 2:14–16). In our sinful madness, we longed for the husks that the swine were eating, but now we are like the Prodigal Son, who, "when he came to him-self . . . said, '. . . I will arise and go to my father'" (Luke 15:17–18). Though at one time we wanted what this world could afford, we have come to say, "Whom have I in heaven but you? And there is nothing on earth that I desire besides you" (Ps. 73:25).

The Most Shocking Passage

In some ways, I think that 2 Peter 1:3–4 is the most shock-ing passage in the whole Bible. If you are thinking about this passage for the first time, or if you have grown accustomed to thinking of yourself as a worm, you might think that it sounds like an idea espoused by a cult, but it is in the Bible.

24. Westminster Shorter Catechism, answer 35.

His divine power has granted to us all things that pertain to life and godliness, through the knowledge of him who called us to his own glory and excellence, by which he has granted to us his precious and very great promises, so that through them you may become partakers of the divine nature, having escaped from the corruption that is in the world because of sinful desire.

You may become partakers of the divine nature. God's power has provided everything that you need for this to happen. When you come to know Jesus Christ, you have embraced a Savior who expects great things of you and who calls you to them. He lived a life of glory and excellence when he was on the earth, and now that he has crossed the finish line, he turns and calls you to a life of glory and excellence. He equips and motivates you with his very great and precious promises. You have become a partaker in the divine nature. You were created in the image of God, but you were bruised and mangled by the fall. You fell into a diseased way of thinking and living, and you were enslaved by the corruption that is in the world because of sinful desire, but your King freed you, and you have escaped. He has adopted you into his family. Your greatest delight is to know him, "and this is eternal life, that they know you, the only true God, and Jesus Christ whom you have sent" (John 17:3) As you behold the glory of the Lord, you "are being transformed into the same image from one degree of glory to another" (2 Cor. 3:18). You are precious in his sight.

You are part of his bride, and he will not let another have you.

Christ loved the church and gave himself up for her, that he might sanctify her, having cleansed her by the washing of water with the word, so that he might present the church to himself in splendor, without spot or wrinkle or any such thing, that she might be holy and without blemish. (Eph. 5:25–27)

You are his child, and he will not give you up.

Can a woman forget her nursing child,
    that she should have no compassion on the son of her
        womb?
Even these may forget,
    yet I will not forget you.
Behold, I have engraved you on the palms of my hands.
      (Isa. 49:15–16)

You are his sheep, he knows you, and he will protect you from the wolf.

I am the good shepherd. I know my own and my own know me, just as the Father knows me and I know the Father; and I lay down my life for the sheep. (John 10:14–15)

You are one of his precious jewels.

They shall be mine, saith the LORD of hosts, in that day when I make up my jewels; and I will spare them, as a man spareth his own son that serveth him. (Mal. 3:17 KJV)

Jesus holds you tight in his strong hand, and he is in the Father's hand.

I give them eternal life, and they will never perish, and no one will snatch them out of my hand. My Father, who has given them to me, is greater than all, and no one is able to snatch them out of the Father's hand. (John 10:28–29)

How could you be in a safer place?

What then shall we say to these things? If God is for us, who can be against us? He who did not spare his own Son but gave him up for us all, how will he not also with him graciously give us all things? Who shall bring any charge against God's elect? It is God who justifies. Who is to condemn? Christ Jesus is the one who died—more than that, who was raised—who is at the right hand of God, who indeed is interceding for us. Who shall separate us from the love of Christ? Shall tribulation, or distress, or persecution, or famine, or nakedness, or danger, or sword? As it is written,

> "For your sake we are being killed all the day long;
> we are regarded as sheep to be slaughtered."

No, in all these things we are more than conquerors through him who loved us. For I am sure that neither death nor life, nor angels nor rulers, nor things present nor things to come, nor powers, nor height nor depth, nor anything else in all creation, will be able to separate us from the love of God in Christ Jesus our Lord. (Rom. 8:31–39)

Questions for Contemplation and Discussion

1. What if someone no longer wants to be a Christian? Will God force that person to remain a Christian?
2. We have all known persons who professed faith in Christ, and seemed sincere, but who later fell away from the faith. Did those people lose their salvation?

3. As you consider the principles laid out in this chapter, how do they apply to the issue of backsliding? How long can backsliding last? When a person is in a backslidden condition, ought she to take comfort in the doctrine of the eternal security of the believer?

4. The Bible writers emphasize that God grants salvation to those who receive Christ. What does the word *Christ* mean? What offices does Christ fulfill, and what does he do in each of the offices? What does it mean to receive Christ in each of his offices?

5. Believing that Christ died for sinners is an essential part of the gospel, but believing this truth, or believing that Christ died for me in particular, is not the same thing as receiving Christ. What is the difference? Is it possible to receive Christ without trusting in him as God's appointed Savior for sinners? Is it possible to receive Christ without believing that God raised him from the dead?

7

WHAT IF?

Less Than the Five Points

What if Christ has not been raised from the dead? The apostle Paul raises this question in 1 Corinthians 15:12–19, and he considers its dire consequences. Among them are that "our preaching is in vain and your faith is vain" (v. 14), "you are still in your sins" (v. 17), "those also who have fallen asleep in Christ have perished" (v. 18), and "we are of all people most to be pitied" (v. 19).

Then the tone of the passage changes from this dirge in a minor key to an anthem in a major key when Paul sings, "*But in fact* Christ has been raised from the dead" (v. 20), and he proceeds to proclaim the results, which may be summarized as "We are telling the truth, and you have believed the truth; your sins are forgiven in Christ; believers who have fallen asleep in death will be raised; and Christ is reigning over all" (vv. 20–28).

In this concluding chapter, I will follow Paul's example and consider a series of *what if* questions, and I will follow up each *what if* section with a section that begins, "*But in fact . . .*"

What If God Is Not Sovereign over All?

In the first chapter I said that Calvinism is more than the five points; in the grander scheme, Calvinism is the belief that God is sovereign over all things and that God does as he pleases. What if this is not true? If God is not sovereign over all, then there are some things, persons, and events that God either cannot or will not control. If that be the case, then future events must be uncertain. The ultimate triumph of Christ is contingent on events that may never happen. Past and present events may be the work of persons or the result of circumstances that God has not controlled. Therefore, we may not legitimately take comfort in believing that there is purpose in our trials and in our sufferings, since they may be instigated and carried along by evil persons or by random sequences of events. The fall into sin, and even the death of Christ, might have been the triumph of Satan in thwarting God's preferences—yes, *preferences*; there can be no decrees. If God is not sovereign over all, then all his plans are contingent on the cooperation of intelligent moral agents who have the capacity to choose something that God could not prevent. We may not receive our inheritance. Christ said, "All authority in heaven and on earth has been given to me" (Matt. 28:18)—but he must have been expressing an unrealistic optimism, since not even God the Father really has all authority. Or at least he does not exercise it.

But in fact God is sovereign over all, "and he does according to his will among the host of heaven and among the inhabitants of the earth; and none can stay his hand or say to him, 'What have you done?'" (Dan. 4:35). Since God is sovereign over all, the ultimate victory of Christ is certain, and loud voices will surely say, "The kingdom of the world has become the kingdom of our Lord and of his Christ, and he shall reign forever and ever" (Rev. 11:15).

We can know that God is in control of our trials and sufferings, "and we know that for those who love God all things work together for good, for those who are called according to his purpose" (Rom. 8:28). The devil may attack us, but he is God's devil and cannot touch us without God's permission (see Job 1).

Our God is the one who says, "I am God, and there is no other; I am God, and there is none like me, declaring the end from the beginning and from ancient times things not yet done, saying 'My counsel shall stand, and I will accomplish all my purpose'" (Isa. 46:9–10). He will accomplish his purpose, and we will receive our inheritance, "having been predestined according to the purpose of him who works all things according to the counsel of his will" (Eph. 1:11). Christ has all authority, for "God has highly exalted him and bestowed on him the name that is above every name" (Phil. 2:9).

We may boldly obey our Lord, who commanded us to

Go therefore and make disciples of all nations, baptizing them in the name of the Father and of the Son and of the Holy Spirit, teaching them to observe all that I have commanded you. And behold, I am with you always, to the end of the age. (Matt. 28:19–20)

The Lord is King! lift up thy voice,
O earth; and all ye heav'ns, rejoice!
From world to world the joy shall ring,
"The Lord omnipotent is king."

The Lord is king! who then shall dare
Resist His will, distrust His care,
Or murmur at His wise decrees,
Or doubt His royal promises?

The Lord is King! Child of the dust,
The Judge of all the earth is just;
Holy and true are all His ways;
Let every creature speak His praise.

He reigns! ye saints, exalt your strains;
Your God is king, your Father reigns;
And He is at the Father's side,
The Man of love, the Crucified.

Come, make your wants, your burdens known;
He will present them at the throne;
And angel bands are waiting there
His messages of love to bear.

O when His wisdom can mistake,
His might decay, His love forsake,
Then may His children cease to sing,
"The Lord omnipotent is king!"[1]

What If Total Depravity Is Not True?

If humans are not totally depraved, then Jesus had to be using hyperbole when he said, "No one can come to me unless the Father who sent me draws him" (John 6:44). Not all natural persons reject the things of the Spirit of God, for to at least some of them those things make sense, and they can discern them without the aid of the Spirit (contrary to 1 Corinthians 2:14). They are not really "dead in . . . trespasses and sins" (Eph. 2:1); they are just sick—maybe the spiritual equivalent of an upset tummy that is easily cured with an

---

1. Josiah Conder, "The Lord Is King," 1824.

over-the-counter dose of an emotional story or a rousing motivational pep talk.

Since everyone has a little spark of good that has the potential to be coaxed into a flame, our aim in evangelism may be directed toward that spark. All psychological *manipu- lation* . . . such a disparaging word—all *psychological techniques of motivation*, let us rather say, are on the table. Sing another stanza of the invitation hymn, and another, and another, and another. Remind them that Jesus has already done all he can do and that they will be doing him a big favor if they will just let him into their hearts. If sinners are to receive Christ, we have got to talk them into it. In fact, all the pressure and responsibility of discovering what will work on sinners falls back on you and me. If sinners are not dead and divine inter- vention is not required, then surely we have something in our first aid kit that will cure the sick.

But in fact humans are totally depraved. They do not have a spiritual tummy ache; they are dead. We must be made alive and drawn to Christ by the Father. As evangelists, we must have nothing to do with techniques of psychological manipulation—such an accurate word—and we are set free to proclaim the gospel of Christ, which is the only message that God uses to raise the dead. God must get all the glory for our own salvation and for the salvation of others, for if he had left us to ourselves, we would have perished.

> Sin, like a venomous disease,
> Infects our vital blood;
> The only balm is sovereign grace,
> And the physician God.
>
> Our beauty and our strength are fled,
> And we draw near to death;

But Christ the Lord recalls the dead
With his almighty breath.

Madness by nature reigns within,
The passions burn and rage;
Till God's own Son, with skill divine,
The inward fire assuage.[2]

What If Unconditional Election Is Not True?

We must believe something about election, since those who wrote the Bible were led by the Holy Spirit to write often about election and predestination. If election is not particular and unconditional, then perhaps it is universal or conditional. If it is universal, then God chose every human and his choosing them is virtually meaningless, since most humans are not eventually saved. If election is conditional, then God's choice of which people are saved is based on foreseen conditions in them, and again election is virtually meaningless since it is no more than a confirmation that those who believe in Christ are worthy to be chosen to be included in his family. In this case, God's choice is merely a reaction and might well be called *conditional reaction* rather than *conditional election*. If unconditional election is not true, then Christ could not be confident that his work would save anyone. He was merely using highly enigmatic, figurative language when he spoke of *those whom the Father had given him*. If the Father had not given him anyone, then it is virtually impossible to figure out what he was saying. If unconditional election is not true, then those of us who evangelize have no basis for any confidence that our efforts will have any effect at all.

2. Isaac Watts, "Sin, Like a Venomous Disease," 1707.

But in fact it is true that God

> chose us in him before the foundation of the world, that we should be holy and blameless before him. In love he predestined us for adoption to himself as sons through Jesus Christ, according to the purpose of his will, to the praise of his glorious grace, with which he has blessed us in the Beloved. (Eph. 1:4–6)

God the Father gave a people to his Son, and Christ could say, "All that the Father gives me will come to me" (John 6:37) and "I am praying for them. I am not praying for the world but for those whom you have given me, for they are yours" (John 17:9). God knew his elect and loved them in eternity past, and "Those whom he foreknew he also predestined to be conformed to the image of his Son" (Rom. 8:29). He chose his people unconditionally, so all praise for our salvation must go to him.

We who speak the gospel may take courage and press on to take the message of Christ into all the world, for we are sure that God has his elect sheep scattered among the nations, and his sheep will hear his voice and follow him. We may enjoy the comfort of knowing that if we believe in Christ, God has loved us with an everlasting love.

> 'Tis not that I did choose thee,
> For, Lord, that could not be;
> This heart would still refuse thee,
> Hadst thou not chosen me.
> Thou from the sin that stained me
> Hast cleansed and set me free;
> Of old thou hast ordained me,
> That I should live to thee.

'Twas sov'reign mercy called me
And taught my op'ning mind;
The world had else enthralled me,
To heav'nly glories blind.
My heart owns none before thee,
For thy rich grace I thirst;
This knowing, if I love thee,
Thou must have loved me first.[3]

What If Limited Atonement Is Not True?

If limited atonement is not true, then Christ's death was something other than a substitutionary penal atonement. If Christ died for every person, and if every person is not saved as a consequence of Christ's death, then Christ was not really their substitute, he did not really suffer their penalty, and, since God is still angry with them, their sins are not atoned for. If Jesus truly did die as a substitute for every person who has ever lived and if some of those people suffer for sins in hell, then God is guilty of the injustice of punishing sins twice. If Christ offered a universal atonement, it theoretically makes the salvation of all persons possible, but that atonement does not make the salvation of even one person certain.

If Jesus died for every person, then it must be something other than Christ's atoning work that distinguishes a saved person from a lost person. Is it my faith? Is it my repentance? How do I know if my faith is strong enough? How do I know if my repentance is deep enough? If my salvation depends the slightest bit on what I do, then I am doomed to perpetual doubt about my standing before God. If Christ died for

3. Josiah Conder, "'Tis Not That I Did Choose Thee," 1836.

all persons, then the success of the gospel depends on the response of those who hear.

But in fact limited atonement is true. Christ paid the penalty for all the sins of his chosen people, and each of them will certainly be saved. God's wrath toward the elect is certain to be propitiated. Christ is a Savior who really saves. He paid a ransom for his captive people, and it was enough. The ransomed are freed from their captivity. When the Holy Spirit speaks about the results of Christ's work, his confident, victorious tone in the New Testament is warranted. It was prophesied that Jesus would save his people from their sins, and he did it. It is not the size of my faith or the sincerity of my repentance that saves me; it is Christ who saves me. I may enjoy assurance of salvation because my salvation depends on the finished work of Christ. We who speak the gospel may proclaim a full salvation to all who will receive Christ the Lord. We gladly join our voices in the new song and sing,

> Worthy are you to take the scroll
>   and to open its seals,
> for you were slain, and by your blood you ransomed people for God
>   from every tribe and language and people and nation,
> and you have made them a kingdom and priests to our God,
>   and they shall reign on the earth. (Rev. 5:9–10)

What If Irresistible Grace Is Not True?

If irresistible grace is not true, then a sinner must be capable of responding to the gospel call, and the work of the Holy Spirit is not really necessary for salvation. If God is determined to save a sinner and the sinner successfully resists God's overtures of grace, then God's purpose is thwarted and the sinner demonstrates that his will is more potent than God's will. If irresistible grace is not true, then Christ's work on behalf of sinners might have been entirely without effect, since it was possible that not even one sinner would have believed on him. There is really no point in praying for God to intervene in the lives of lost people. He would not invade the sanctity of their free will, so why ask? You would not want God to give anyone an unfair advantage, and to be fair he must either leave everyone alone or else draw everyone equally.

If a sinner does come to Christ, it is ultimately because something in the sinner enabled him to reject the sin that he loves and embrace a sin-killing Christ whom he hates—all of which is contrary to his nature. If a sinner has this capability in him, then either the new birth is unnecessary or he is able to give himself the new birth. As evangelists, we are responsible to stir up this supernatural capability—which, since it can be exercised without supernatural aid, is not supernatural at all.

But *in fact* irresistible grace is true. You were incapable of coming to Christ on your own, so if you have come to him, you know that the Father drew you. The Father elected you, the Son died for you, and the Holy Spirit has called you with a holy calling. The Holy Spirit has informed your thoughts, redirected your affections, and renewed your will. He gave you the new birth, opened your blinded eyes, and raised you from the dead. Even now you have eternal life, and you are being prepared to enjoy eternal life in heaven. As evangelists, we may share the gospel knowing that the sovereign Lord will draw his elect to the Savior, for "those whom he predestined he also called" (Rom. 8:30).

> I sought the Lord, and afterward I knew
> He moved my soul to seek him, seeking me;

It was not I that found, O Savior true,
No, I was found of thee.

Thou didst reach forth thy hand and mine enfold;
I walked and sank not on the storm-vexed sea—
'Twas not so much that I on thee took hold,
As thou, dear Lord, on me.

I find, I walk, I love, but O the whole
Of love is but my answer, Lord, to thee;
For thou wert long beforehand with my soul,
Always thou lovedst me.[4]

What If the Perseverance of the Saints Is Not True?

If God does not preserve his people and enable them to persevere to the end, then no one's salvation is secure. You may be sailing on the sea of salvation today, but who knows what unexpected gust of temptation will prove too strong for you to withstand, and tomorrow you may be hopelessly blown off course and lost forever.

If a person can lose his salvation, how much sin does it take to make him lost? Is one sin enough? Does God require you to make a full confession of every sin if you are to remain in good standing with him? What if you have sins of which you are unaware? How can you confess what you do not know? If God is not preserving you, then who is? It must be you. You have got to keep yourself saved. If you can lose your salvation because of what you do, you must have had some part in getting your salvation, because if your salvation

4. Anonymous, "I Sought the Lord, and afterward I Knew," 1878.

depends totally on Christ's finished work, that can never be altered.

But if you can lose your salvation, then you will not know whether you are going to heaven until after you die. If you do make it to heaven, you will deserve at least part of the glory for your salvation, because you held out faithful. You will be in heaven not because God preserved you but because you just had what it takes. Meanwhile, as an evangelist, you cannot honestly promise eternal life to those who repent and believe, because whatever kind of life believers receive, it is not really eternal if it can be lost.

But in fact God does preserve his people forever. Winds of temptation may blow, but the Master of Storms is in your little boat, and he will guide you safely into the harbor. Your sins do not take God by surprise; all your sins were future and were all known to him when his Son paid the bloody price of your ransom. At the cross, God's justice was satisfied and his wrath against you was propitiated. When you received Christ, you were united to him, and Christ will never die again because of sin. Neither will you. He has been raised, and you have been raised with him. You are saved because of the finished work of Christ. The Father loved you in eternity past, and he chose you to be his own. Christ took you to be part of his bride. The Holy Spirit clothed you in the wedding garment of the righteousness of Christ. You will be in heaven on that day when the marriage supper of the Lamb takes place, and you will not be a mere spectator or even a bridesmaid. You will be part of the bride.

> I saw a poor, poor woman, and clothed with rags was she,
> So full of dark uncleanness and foul impurity,
> With wounds and bruises grievous and sins of crimson red—
> A stench to God Almighty, and in trespasses dead.
> Unrighteous, filthy rags were all she had to wear.

I saw the King of glory come from his throne on high
To save his chosen people, and for a bride to die,
Clothed in his robes of righteousness, so pure and holy he—
The joy of God his Father through all eternity.
A crown of cruel thorns was what he came to wear.

The woman heard of Jesus and trembled in despair;
She gazed upon her garment—each gaping, ragged tear;
She wept in deep contrition and deep repentance too;
It was her sin that clothed her so, and this the women knew.
Unholy sin-strained rags were all she had to wear.

The King came to the woman and called her by her name,
But she did weep and hide her face and hang her head in
      shame.
He told her of his love for her and how he gave his life
To save her from her sinfulness and take her for his wife.
God's holy wrath for her was what he came to bear.

"Dear Lord," she cried in gratitude, "why have you chosen
      me?"
"To show my love and grace," he said, "throughout
      eternity."
"But Lord," said she, "I am not fit! What of my filthy clothes?"
He said, "Put on my righteousness, and you must give me
      those."
Her sins, upon the cross, were what he came to bear.

I saw them on their wedding day—the morn of endless time:
The poor, poor woman shining bright in righteousness
      divine.
What praises, from the multitude, like peals of thunder
      rang!

The hosts of heaven cried aloud, and this is what they sang:
Fine linen, bright and clean, was given her to wear.[5]

What Now?

If the Lord has revealed to you the truths taught in this book, then what now? Many pastors conclude their sermons with a section that consists of several points of application. The idea is a biblical one. Paul often began his letters with theological teaching and concluded them with practical application. When he begins the practical application in his letter to the Romans, he writes,

> I appeal to you therefore, brothers, by the mercies of God, to present your bodies as a living sacrifice, holy and acceptable to God, which is your spiritual worship. Do not be conformed to this world, but be transformed by the renewal of your mind, that by testing you may discern what is the will of God, what is good and acceptable and perfect. (Rom. 12:1–2)

When your mind has been renewed by the truth, the foundational step of transformation has been taken. It may take some time, but eventually a renewed mind will transform all of life.

Belief in the Five Points of Calvinism ought to transform us. It cultivates humility as we come to understand that we had nothing to do with our salvation. "Then what becomes of our boasting? It is excluded" (Rom. 3:27). It produces

5. In 1984 I was reading Revelation, and I read in 19:8, "Fine linen, bright and clean, was given her to wear" (NIV). I asked myself, "What was she wearing before?" The idea for this poem came to me at once, and within a few days I wrote this poem and set it to music.

gratitude. When we see the deep, stinking swamp of our sin, we gain a fresh appreciation for the vast, pristine mountain of God's grace. We feel a fresh love for God. He chose us when we were unworthy. Christ died for us when we were without strength. The Holy Spirit wisely and powerfully overcame our resistance and drew us to Christ. We are saved from hell, and we are going to heaven because of him! Knowing that we have been forgiven much, we love much.

When we believe the Five Points, we are better situated to glorify God and enjoy him forever.[6] We give all glory to God for our salvation. Not one bit of credit can go to us. God has revealed himself to us as our loving Father, Christ is our dear Redeemer, and the Holy Spirit is our faithful Comforter. We are reconciled to God, and we have been born again

> to an inheritance that is imperishable, undefiled, and unfading, kept in heaven for you, who by God's power are being guarded through faith for a salvation ready to be revealed in the last time. . . . Though you have not seen him, you love him. Though you do not now see him, you believe in him and rejoice with joy that is inexpressible and filled with glory, obtaining the outcome of your faith, the salvation of your souls. (1 Peter 1:4–5, 8–9)

Questions for Contemplation and Discussion

1. God is sovereign over all persons and all events, including the sinful deeds of humans and the natural disasters that cause death and destruction. How can God be good and allow all these things to happen?

2. "We know that for those who love God all things work

6. See the Westminster Shorter Catechism, answer 1.

together for good" (Rom. 8:28). Do all things work together for good for those who do not love God?

3. What is the difference between fate and God's sovereignty?

4. Surprisingly, when an awakened sinner understands the doctrine of total depravity, he may experience a great calm. Why?

5. Some presume that the elect must be proud of the fact that God chose them. Why is this an unfounded presumption? What ought to be the attitude of the elect?

6. "God loves you, and Jesus died for you, but that will not save you." Is this a true statement? Why, or why not?

7. Many pastors conclude their worship service with an "altar call," inviting persons to come forward for various reasons. There is neither command nor example of this in the Bible. Is it a helpful practice?

8. Does the doctrine of the perseverance of the saints tend to make Christians lazy in their pursuit of holiness?

AFTERWORD

I dedicated this book to my uncle Paul A. Orrick. On January 1, 1980, I was on my way back to college after Christmas break, and I stopped in Mt. Vernon, Illinois, to spend the night with my grandmother, Mamaw. Uncle Paul lived next door, and I walked over to see him. He and I sat at his kitchen table and discussed the gospel. I was nineteen years old. I had been a believer for five years, and I had already been preaching for over a year, but God used a couple of things that he said that night to give me a clearer understanding of the gospel than I had before. He said, "The sinner's cry is not, 'Okay, Jesus, I am going to let you come into my heart and save me.' Instead, the sinner's cry is, in the words of Fanny Crosby's hymn,

Pass me not, O gentle Savior!
Hear my humble cry.
While on others thou art calling,
Do not pass me by."[1]

That came home to my heart then, and even now, as I type these words nearly forty years later, tears well up in my eyes.

1. Fanny J. Crosby, "Pass Me Not, O Gentle Savior," 1868.

Uncle Paul told me about an encounter that he had with a preacher who pastored in the same town as he did. He happened to meet the other preacher in the grocery store, and he said, "Orrick, we ought to get our churches together for a meeting."

My uncle replied, "We cannot do that."

He asked why.

Uncle Paul said, "Because you preach a different gospel than I do." (He is so subtle.)

When the preacher inquired how their gospels were different, Uncle Paul asked him, "Tell me this: why are you going to heaven?"

The man replied, "Because I believe in Jesus."

Now, that is not a wrong answer. It is a pretty decent answer. The Lord does promise salvation to those who believe in him. But my uncle wanted to make a point with him, so he said to him, "That is the difference between the gospels that you and I preach. When you answered my question, the first words out of your mouth were 'Because I.' The gospel that I preach requires that when I answer the question 'Why are you going to heaven?' the first words out of my mouth must be 'Because He.'"

In the first chapter of this book, I told a story about an encounter I had in which someone asked me to summarize Calvinism in two sentences, and I tried to accomplish this. My uncle did better than that. He summarized it in only two words: "Because He."

I walked over to Mamaw's that night. She was already in bed, and the house was quiet. I went back into the freezing cold back bedroom where I was staying, and I lay down on an old, rickety cot, but I could not sleep—not because it was so cold, but because my heart was on fire with the gospel of sovereign grace: the blessed gospel that has been summarized in this book. There was a huge lump in my throat as I lay in that dark room and realized, like never before, *I am saved because of what Jesus has already done! This changes everything!*

And it has. Oh, it has.

More from P&R Publishing

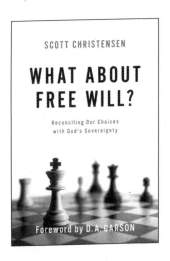

SCOTT CHRISTENSEN

WHAT ABOUT FREE WILL?

Reconciling Our Choices with God's Sovereignty

Foreword by D. A. CARSON

Free will is a complex topic, but the Bible is clear: God's absolute sovereignty exists alongside our free, responsible choices. Only one view, *compatibilism*, fully embraces this truth.

Making a fresh, scriptural case for compatibilism, Scott Christensen explains the issues involved and addresses arguments on both sides. His absorbing pastoral analysis will help you to develop a new appreciation for the role your choices play in God's sovereign plans and to better understand the Bible's views on evil and suffering, prayer, evangelism, sanctification, and more.

"A clear, intelligent, immensely helpful overview of one of the most confusing conundrums in all of theology. . . . Scott Christensen doesn't sidestep the hard questions. The answers he gives are thoughtful, biblical, satisfying, and refreshingly coherent. Lay readers and seasoned theologians alike will treasure this work."
—**John F. MacArthur**, Grace Community Church

More from P&R Publishing

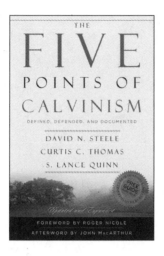

An introduction of the five points of Calvinism that defines, defends, and documents these doctrines that form the basic framework of God's plan for saving sinners.

After describing the history and contents of Calvinism and contrasting its points with the "five points of Arminianism," the authors supply verses to form a biblical defense of the doctrine before finally laying out additional resources to encourage and aid readers to make their own thorough investigation of Calvinistic theology.

"One could hardly wish for a better study resource to show the five points' faithfulness to Scripture."
—J. I. Packer

"Truly a classic—clear, concise, and warm in its presentation of historic Reformed theology."
—R.C. Sproul

"My thanks to P&R Publishing for issuing . . . this excellent book."
—Joni Eareckson Tada